# EVANGELISM
## AND PAGAN ENGLAND

# EVANGELISM
## AND PAGAN ENGLAND

by

J. ERNEST RATTENBURY

WIPF & STOCK · Eugene, Oregon

Wipf and Stock Publishers
199 W 8th Ave, Suite 3
Eugene, OR 97401

Evangelism and Pagan England
By Rattenbury, J. Ernest
Copyright©1954 Methodist Publishing - Epworth Press
ISBN 13: 978-1-5326-4004-9
Publication date 9/2/2017
Previously published by Epworth Press, 1954

Every effort has been made to trace the current copyright
owner of this publication but without success. If you have
any information or interest in the copyright, please contact the publishers.

DEDICATED
TO
Dr DONALD O. SOPER
*President of the Methodist Conference*
(1953-4)
WHOSE THOUGHT-EVOKING PREACHING,
DAUNTLESS COURAGE, INSPIRING LEADERSHIP
AND AFFECTIONATE FRIENDSHIP
HAVE IN MY OLD AGE BEEN TO ME AS
'LIGHT AT EVENTIDE'

## AUTHOR'S NOTE

I AM most grateful to friends who have helped me in the production of this book, and especially to my nephew, the Rev. Morley Rattenbury, M.A., who read my typescript and gave me some valuable suggestions, for which I thank him. I am also under deep obligation to Miss Marjorie Harry, Miss Esther Broadbent, Miss Doris Hardy, Miss Dorothy Williams and Mr T. A. Herbert Bilsby, M.A., to whom I give my thanks. I have pleasure also in acknowledging the permission of Ernest Benn Ltd to quote at length from *Dreams*, by Olive Schreiner.

J. E. R.

# CONTENTS

INTRODUCTION . . . . . . . . 1

## Part One
### Autobiographical Reflections on Evangelism

1  THE OLD EVANGELISM . . . . . . 9
2  REFLECTIONS OF AN OCTOGENARIAN
   (I) EVANGELISTIC REGRESSION . . . . 22
3  REFLECTIONS OF AN OCTOGENARIAN
   (II) A METHODIST REVIVAL WITH A NEW NOTE . 31
4  REFLECTIONS OF AN OCTOGENARIAN
   (III) THE EXPERIENCES OF AN EVANGELIST . . 42

## Part Two
### The Twofold Gospel: the Kingdom and the Church

5  THE GOOD NEWS . . . . . . . 53
6  THE TWOFOLD GOSPEL . . . . . . 63
7  THE CHRISTIAN REVOLUTION . . . . 72
8  THE FAMILY OF GOD . . . . . . 87

## Part Three
### The Modern Situation and Evangelism

9   THEN AND NOW . . . . . . . 103
10  MODERN DIFFICULTIES FOR EVANGELISTS . . . 113
11  THE CHRISTIAN ANSWER TO THE MODERN CHALLENGE 122
12  'ATTEND THE TRUMPET'S SOUND!' . . . 134
    ADDITIONAL NOTE: ESCHATOLOGY AND APOCALYPTIC 143

*What we have felt and seen*
*With confidence we tell,*
*And publish to the sons of men*
*The signs infallible.*

## INTRODUCTION

EVANGELISM is a much wider term than Methodism, but it may I think be justly claimed that Methodism is the outstanding historical result of the Evangelical Revival of the eighteenth century. The movement is the mother at least amongst English-speaking people of most modern evangelistic appeals. Since one must begin somewhere I begin with the Church with which I am most familiar.

I confess that in recent years I have been dissatisfied with the results of evangelistic campaigns often widely publicized. While the effort of world Methodism in 1953 has obtained in some places good results, and the effort and devotion of many Methodists has been admirable and assuredly will be crowned with success in days to come, it must be acknowledged, as Dr Soper said in his Presidential address, that the revival has not come. As I look back on the many evangelistic campaigns of the last sixty to seventy years I cannot but conclude that their apparent results have been a diminishing quantity. Reflection upon these facts is largely responsible for the following pages, in which I deal exclusively with the English situation. Of world evangelization I am not competent to speak, but if Latourette is to be believed, the expansion of Christianity throughout the world in our own times is one to encourage the Church.

In recent years the most immediately successful appeals of this type seem to have been by Fundamentalist organizations. The dogmatic statement of a few plain doctrines such as those of the 'Four-Square Gospel' seem to appeal to great numbers of people. It is no valid criticism of these appeals to say that the people who respond to them are generally illiterate, as the same criticisms could be made of the early Christian Church and the Methodist Revival of the eighteenth century. The Fundamentalist never makes the mistake so often made by 'modernists' of supposing that the modern man is only modern, whereas the most striking fact about any modern people in every age is their likeness to Adam and Eve. Our similarities with the people of the past are much more striking than our differences from them. As Goethe said: 'Mankind is always advancing and man always remains the same.' In the teaching of such movements there is nothing strikingly novel except in some cases a doctrine of 'healing', but the direct appeal of the Gospel to the human hearts of those people whose minds are blind to the new problems of our age is effective and always will be. Such teaching is simple, intelligible, dogmatic, and unqualified. These are important features in popular appeal.

Though in these pages I shall try to show how the appeal of the Gospel is affected by modern thinking and to emphasize elements of it most likely to appeal to the people of our own age, I can never forget the fundamental needs of human nature which do not vary from age to age. It is difficult to think, notwithstanding the immediate successes of Fundamentalist appeal, that an appeal which is so blind to the new knowledge of our times can be of great permanent value. The success of the appeal of Roman Catholicism is probably due to similar conditions. A plain unqualified dogmatic teaching undoubtedly has great immediate advantage.

Twenty years ago I wrote a book entitled *Evangelism, Its Shame and Glory*. It was an appeal to Methodists, at the time when the separate Methodist bodies were about to unite, that they would unitedly return to their first love, Evangelism. The book has long been out of print although I have been not infrequently requested to republish it. I never felt that I could do so without rewriting much of it (written as it was for a special purpose), and giving it a more general application. Furthermore, certain statements and arguments in the book were the result of controversy, as to the meaning and application of the word 'evangelism'. I tried to answer writings which seemed to me to take all distinctive meaning out of the term. Though this was not difficult I feel now that my definition of the Gospel was too restricted. While the positive statements of the book need no alteration and my general conviction of the necessity and methods of evangelism remain unchanged, I am glad that I did not republish it, especially as I have come to realize that there are features of evangelism of great moment for our own times, which were lacking in the evangelical appeal of the Wesleys.

I believe intensely in the old evangelical appeal to the individual, and that the Pauline Gospel of which the great Apostle was not ashamed, because it was the power of God to salvation, will always be effective, so long as it is true, as it always must be, that

> *Never morning wore*
> *To evening, but some heart did break.*

It is necessary, however, to realize more than perhaps has been done in evangelical circles, that beneath the individual Gospel appeal of St Paul, there lies the appeal, not only individual but collective, in the Gospel of Jesus, as expressed by his good news of the coming of the Kingdom of God.

I have divided this book into three parts. In the first, after a brief statement of the values and defects of the Evangelical Movement of the eighteenth century, I have set down a number of personal reflections and experiences of evangelism.

I have often, on account I suppose, of my long and varied experiences of Methodism and of my family relations to an older evangelism, been asked to write an autobiography. While I am not prepared to do this, I have so far complied with the request as to give some account of my own experiences as an Evangelist and to write reflections on the Evangelistic Movement of the last seventy years, because I think that this may be the most vital approach to a treatment of the evangelism needed for our own days.

In the second part, since I believe the message of the evangelist is much more important than his method, I have attempted to state the gospel both of individual salvation and the Kingdom of God. I have added chapters dealing on the principles on which the City of God is to be built, and on the Church as the Divine Society by which these principles can be carried out.

In the third part I have accepted as the best analysis I know of the modern situation, the Presidential speech of Doctor Donald Soper at the Methodist Conference of 1953, and have tried to show by a series of contrasts between 'Now and Then' the adaptations necessary for effective evangelism in our own days. In these later chapters I have recurred to some extent to my autobiographical method.

Some of my readers may think that chapters 5 to 8 are different in tone from other chapters of this book and rather irrelevant to the general treatment of practical evangelism. This, however, is not so. The message that the evangelist of today must deliver is more important than the method of its delivery. The absence of the Gospel—the good news—of the Kingdom from the old evangelical appeal was a defect, not perhaps a conspicuous defect under the conditions of the eighteenth century. But now that the social obligations of the Church have become increasingly apparent in our own times, I believe that emphasis upon social implications of Christ's teaching is the only possible effective reply to the claims of Communism and like modern movements.

Dr Dodd's statement of 'Realized Eschatology' seems to me the most important contribution to Biblical Theology of our time. When this statement is accepted as true, as I accept it, the inferences which I have made, and expressed in my views of the Kingdom of Christ on earth, must not be supposed to be those of Dr Dodd. For all I know he may regard my deductions as a building of hay and straw upon the foundations he has laid.

Other readers of this book, will, I expect, criticize the little consideration given to sin and redemption. If it were a general treatment of theology this criticism would be sound and any case needs attention. It is not, as page 81 shows, that I regard the question lightly. Schemes for future evangelization would indeed be futile dreams if the tragedy of human sin were ignored. In some way or other the slumbering sense of guilt in our times must be reawakened, but can this be by antiquated and in certain ways discredited earlier methods of evangelism? The hangover of Puritan negations hampers the modern evangelist. Our age needs a positive religion. I believe that the declaration of the full Gospel as I have tried to detail it, is more likely to awaken a sense of sin than too much dwelling upon the fact. While the last thing I desire is to ignore the existence of sin and personal guilt and the power of Christ to redeem men from their sins, never forgetting the faithful saying that Jesus Christ came into the world to save sinners, I do take all this for granted. I do not believe that the picture of the burdened pilgrim fleeing from the city of destruction will appeal to many men today. Too much thought about sin develops a morbidity which is dangerous to the sinner. The Gospel of Jesus was joyful news and the best message to our age if we can get it across is: 'Hark! the glad sound, the Saviour comes!'

May I venture to add one personal note. I write this book in my eighty-third year as a practical evangelist, thankful to God for blessings which rested upon my own preaching of the

*old, old story*
*Of Jesus and His love,*

but with an enriched sense of the implications of what that story and that love mean. I can of course in my advanced age never hope to practise what I preach here; but if it were possible to begin again, while I would never neglect the individual message of salvation inherited from the Wesleys and ultimately from St Paul, I would try to apply to modern conditions the even older good news of Jesus which I do not think for a moment his great Apostle ever ignored, that the Kingdom of God has arrived.

PART ONE

# AUTOBIOGRAPHICAL REFLECTIONS ON EVANGELISM

*Sinners, obey the gospel word;*
*Haste to the supper of my Lord!*
*Be wise to know your gracious day;*
*All things are ready, come away!*

*Ready the Father is to own*
*And kiss His late-returning son;*
*Ready your loving Saviour stands,*
*And spreads for you His bleeding hands.*

*Ready the Spirit of His love*
*Just now the hardness to remove,*
*To apply, and witness with the blood,*
*And wash and seal the sons of God.*

*Ready for you the angels wait,*
*To triumph in your blest estate;*
*Tuning their harps, they long to praise*
*The wonders of redeeming grace.*

*The Father, Son, and Holy Ghost*
*Is ready, with the shining host;*
*All heaven is ready to resound:*
*The dead's alive, the lost is found!*

*O come, ye sinners, to your Lord,*
*In Christ to paradise restored;*
*His proffered benefits embrace,*
*The plenitude of gospel grace:*

*A pardon written with His blood,*
*The favour and the peace of God,*
*The seeing eye, the feeling sense,*
*The mystic joys of penitence;*

*The godly grief, the pleasing smart,*
*The meltings of a broken heart,*
*The tears that tell your sins forgiven,*
*The sighs that waft your souls to heaven;*

*The guiltless shame, the sweet distress,*
*The unutterable tenderness,*
*The genuine, meek humility,*
*The wonder—Why such love to me?*

*The o'erwhelming power of saving grace,*
*The sight that veils the seraph's face;*
*The speechless awe that dares not move,*
*And all the silent heaven of love.*

CHAPTER ONE

# THE OLD EVANGELISM

A DESIRE to flee from the wrath to come and to be saved from their sins were the two and the only two conditions demanded by John Wesley from candidates for membership of his Society. The wrath to come, that is to say, the Hell of everlasting burning, dominated the thought both of teachers and people in the eighteenth century, and created conditions for evangelism which hardly exist in ours. In the eighteenth century there were no doubt a large number of intellectuals to whom Hell meant nothing. Intellectually it was a sceptical age, and the favourite theme of the 'savants' of the time was the rational character of Christianity. The rejection of the supernatural by the Deists influenced the teaching of the Church. Charles Wesley characterized some of the Bishops of the day as 'mitred infidels'. But such views did not influence the masses to whom the Wesleys preached. The belief in Hell in its material fires and its medieval horrors was general, and probably the Calvinistic preaching of the time that only a few elect persons could escape it, would make multitudes of people accept what they regarded as their fate, and thus become hardened, and careless. Both the Wesleys believed in such a Hell. The most objectionable thing that John Wesley ever wrote was his sermon on Hell, which is quite incredibly horrible; fortunately it was not one of his Standard Doctrinal Sermons. It was a subject on which generally he spoke very little, but it remained in the background of his mind and undoubtedly influenced his preaching of deliverance and salvation.

Charles Wesley, like his brother, believed in Hell, but apparently was sparing in his references to it in his preaching. Curiously enough, it is in his hymns for children that he preaches in quite repulsive terms this doctrine. I suppose he felt that by such teaching children could be frightened into good conduct. It is almost incredible that the man who wrote such a simple and beautiful children's hymn as

> *Gentle Jesus, meek and mild,*
> *Look upon a little child—*

could have written the following grotesque and terrifying lines for children:

> *Shall I, amidst a ghastly band,*
> *Dragg'd to the Judgement-seat*
> *Far on the left with horror stand,*
> *My fearful doom to meet?*
>
> *While they enjoy His heavenly love,*
> *Must I in torment dwell?*
> *And howl (while they sing hymns above),*
> *And blow the flames of hell?*

These words are quite exceptional and uncharacteristic of Charles Wesley's general teaching. Some of his most poignant penitential verses deal with Hell, but deal with it as an experience of a penitential man distressed by his own failures and sins. He writes, for instance, no doubt in reference to some moral tragedy in his own life and experience:

> *I need not fear the burning pool,*
> *Already kindled in my soul,*
> *The wrath Divine I feel.*

But he believed in a love 'stronger than death and Hell' and so sang:

> *My refuge is this*
> *Unexhausted abyss;*
> *Forsaken of all,*
> *Lord, into Thy ocean of mercy I fall.*
> *Here, Jesu, am I*
> *Determined to lie,*
> *Thy goodness to prove,*
> *And if I am lost, to be lost in Thy love.*

It is not often explicitly, at least, in the teaching of the two brothers that we find special emphasis upon Hell, although the fact as they conceive it is in the background of all their thinking and speaking. The Love of God which Charles Wesley, at the time of his conversion especially, speaks of as 'amazing love', *really* amazes him, because he was

> *A brand plucked from eternal fire,*

and the most typical teaching of the Wesleys of God's infinite love would be less intense if it were not thought of in the terms of the merciful and unexpected deliverance from the impending doom of Hell.

It is rather in the lives of the early Methodist Preachers that the eighteenth-century horror and fear of Hell becomes conspicuously apparent. A considerable number of these men reponded to the demand of John Wesley that they should write the story of their lives, and it is clear that the fear of Hell drove them to religion and also equally clear that it was the fear of Hell for others that gave such tremendous earnestness to their teaching, so that they sang a hymn that Charles Wesley wrote for them which expressed their passion for 'souls':

> *I want an even strong desire,*
> *I want a calmly fervent zeal,*
> *To save poor souls out of the fire,*
> *To snatch them from the verge of Hell.*

These men preached Hell so much that John Wesley definitely discouraged them from doing so and instructed them to preach on the Love not the Wrath of God and, no doubt, it was the proclamation of the free unrestricted offer of the love of God to all men however sinful they were, which made their appeal so successful. Their preaching was backed by their personal experience of the pardoning mercy of God. It was dogmatic and unqualified and backed by their own experience, so that people were enormously impressed when these men sang:

> *What we have felt and seen*
> *With confidence we tell,*
> *And publish to the sons of men*
> *The signs infallible.*

What were the facts which humanly speaking made the evangelical appeal to the England of the eighteenth century so effective? Some of them quite plainly recur in the time in which we live. The most notable seem to be:

(1) the fear of Hell with the message of pardoning love which enabled the men who sought Christ to escape from their impending doom;

(2) the impression made on the public mind by the open-air preaching of the two brothers and George Whitefield, dignified university men and priests of the Church of England, had by its novelty an extraordinary influence;

(3) the earnest exhortations of the early Methodist Preachers, themselves the living witnesses of the truths the Wesleys had enunciated;

(4) the thrilling effect of the singing of the hymns of Charles Wesley.

Except for metrical psalms, the singing of hymns was not the custom of the Church in the eighteenth century. The hymns of Charles Wesley set to popular tunes and expressing the truths of the Evangelical Revival with a force and beauty which made them, as they continued to be, the best medium of the Wesleyan theology, did as much, probably more, as the preaching and writing of John Wesley to influence the minds of the people. The open-air preaching of John Wesley was always of a dignified and reverent character. He never preached, for instance, except in academic robes. His preaching though popular was quiet and restrained. The substance of his appeal was re-expressed in the hymns of Charles Wesley, which were the means of giving wings to his brother's doctrines, and which have been more enduring in their theological influence than any other medium of Evangelical teaching.

One of these hymns, printed at the beginning of this chapter, is especially significant. It commences with the words: 'Sinners, obey the Gospel word.' Unfortunately, in our current *Methodist Hymn-book* the hymn has been divided into two parts and, for some inexplicable reason, the second part has been put first (Hymn No. 325) and the first part second (Hymn No. 326).

A reference to this hymn (see page 8, *supra*) will show the character of the Wesleys' preaching. It is based upon the doctrine of the Holy Trinity—the subject is 'All things are now ready', and Charles Wesley combines the parable of the 'Marriage Feast' with the feast given to the returning child in the parable of the Prodigal Son. He shows how God is ready to receive returning sinners with the gladness with which the Father receives his Prodigal son, but it is God in Three Persons

> *Ready the Father is to own*
> *And kiss His late-returning son;*
> *Ready your loving Saviour stands,*
> *And spreads for you His bleeding hands.*
>
> *Ready the Spirit of His Love*
> *Just now the hardness to remove,*

and then in the fifth verse we read:

> *The Father, Son, and Holy Ghost*
> *Is ready.*

The significant fact is that where the ear expects Father, Son, and Holy Ghost *are* ready, the word actually used should be *is*, emphasizing the fact that it is *One* God in Three Persons. The theological precision of this is a notable and unusual feature in a hymn for open-air appeal. One beautiful touch in the hymn is the preparation of the heavenly hosts to rejoice over one sinner that repenteth. So we read in the fourth verse,

> *Ready for you the angels wait,*
> *To triumph in your blest estate;*
> *Tuning their harps . . .*

This picture of the heavenly orchestra preparing, as it were, to sing the Hallelujah Chorus over returning sinners, is to my mind particularly attractive. One can imagine the trumpeters on the other side getting their trumpets ready to join with the angels: in their longing

> *to praise*
> *The wonders of redeeming grace.*

The second part of this hymn (No. 325) gives an account of the heavenly joys which penitent people will share. When one thinks of the 'harlots, publicans and thieves' to whom Charles Wesley in his 'Conversion' hymn makes his appeal, the quality and substance of this hymn is extraordinary. How, one wonders, can such people be attracted by

> *The seeing eye, the feeling sense,*
> *The mystic joys of penitence.*
>
> *The godly grief, the pleasing smart,*
> *The meltings of a broken heart.*
>
> *The guiltless shame, the sweet distress.*
>
> *The o'erwhelming power of saving grace,*
> *The sight that veils the seraph's face;*
> *The speechless awe that dares not move,*
> *And all the silent heaven of love.*

Mystic joys and silent heavens, the fruits of penitence, are not the attractions that open-air evangelists would promise to their hearers today, any more than they would base their appeals on the doctrine of the Trinity. But was it not the rare quality of the doctrine and the deeply spiritual character of such verses as these, which gave permanence and not merely transitory values to the evangelical appeal of the eighteenth century?

Although the singing of such hymns, not only on account of their quality but also because of their novelty, made a unique impression, we must not forget that the authority with which the preachers impressed their hearers was based on Holy Scriptures.

## THE OLD EVANGELISM

The Bible in the last resort was always appealed to as a final authority, and was accepted as such. Its infallibility, and by that I mean the inerrancy of the letter of Scripture, was assumed by the Wesleys and never challenged by their hearers. It must be admitted that John Wesley's attitude to the Bible was sometimes superstitious. Notwithstanding the fact that he was a pioneer in textual criticism and suggested corrections which were accepted by the Revisers of the New Testament in 1881, and spoke of the *Psalter* as containing passages 'highly improper for the lips of a Christian congregation', he held the book in such superstitious reverence that he expected the guidance of the Spirit on any page when he quite casually, although with prayer, opened the book.

It is impossible in our times to treat the letter of Scripture in the manner in which John Wesley treated it. He regarded all Scriptures as of equal value with no sense of distinction of one author from another. Any sentence or clause, which he found in the Scripture was to him literally sacred. Sometimes his use of Scripture sentences, as for instance in the long letter he wrote to William Law, are irritating and unconvincing. People read the Bible very little today, which is to be much regretted since modern knowledge has made the sacred Book as a whole far more intelligible than it has ever been. When the new interpretations of Scripture filter down into the mind of the people, Bible teaching, though different in style, may well be not less effective.

In summary we may say:

(*a*) The main teachings of the Wesleys, effective as they were in the eighteenth century, need a different emphasis today. It is quite clear that the old appeal, 'flee from the wrath to come', can hardly be hopefully used by twentieth-century evangelists. The appeal the Wesleys made was purely individual. While the direct appeal to individual men is a permanent fact in all evangelism, the modern sense that a man only becomes a person through his social relationships is much more clearly understood today than it was in the time of the Wesleys. They had no sense of the social implications of the Kingdom of God. To John Wesley the Kingdom of God was an interior matter of the soul. He interpreted it as righteousness, peace and joy, to use the Pauline expression. The Kingdom of Heaven was an inward experience. 'Seek ye first the Kingdom of God,' for instance, Wesley says, means 'seek it in your heart'. He even interprets the words 'Thy Kingdom come' as 'Thy Kingdom in my heart'.[1] He does, however, teach the future coming of the Kingdom of God in an eschatological sense.

(b) The appeal of the Wesleys was largely negative, so far as it was an evangelical appeal. By negative, I mean it was an appeal to flee *from* the wrath of God and to be saved *from* sin. Doctor E. H. Sugden has criticized somewhat trenchantly John Wesley's conception of sin. He says that Wesley thought of it as if it were a rotten tooth to be extracted. While the illustration is a little crude, it is not without force. Wesley for instance had little sense of the sins of omission with which our Lord dealt so ruthlessly. This negative emphasis, as well as the individual appeal, needs some qualification as will be seen later.

(c) While the appeal of the Wesleys had a sound doctrinal basis and was evident especially in the preaching of John Wesley, intellectual and logical, there was a considerable emotional factor in it. A plea to flee from the wrath to come and to accept the offer of the love of God in Christ, particularly in His death on the Cross, could not be other than emotional. One can well understand how greatly the masses were moved by the dramatic eloquence of George Whitefield and by the poetic raptures of Charles Wesley, but it is difficult to understand when one reads the sermons of John with their close reasoning and literary quality, that they should stir people to emotional response. So far as we can understand, but exact information is largely lacking, the preaching of John Wesley was calm and unexcited, yet there evidently was something in his piercing eye that exercised a power of fascination on his hearers. The emotional and hysterical outbursts of the crowd curiously enough

[1] *Standard Sermons of John Wesley*, I.436.

were more frequent under John Wesley's preaching than under Whitefield's or Charles Wesley's. Charles Wesley indeed suppressed extravagant demonstrations and attributed them to the devil; John Wesley, on the other hand, at least in his earlier preaching, tended to see in them a divine movement. But whatever one thinks of the emotional appeal, the basis of the theological doctrine must not be forgotten.

When the individualistic negative and emotional characteristics of the evangelical appeal are asserted, the assertion must be qualified by the fact of Wesley's careful teaching and practical social service to the people whom he had gathered together in his Societies. The social practice of Wesley and his teaching of perfect love were factors in his work which neutralized the dangers of exclusively individualistic and negative teaching. Indeed, the positive elements required in modern evangelical appeal were implicit in the teachings and practice of the Wesleys even if they were not explicit. The outcast population which responded to their appeal created problems which John Wesley never evaded, but which he tried to solve as they arose. He was profoundly moved by the ill-health and poverty of the people who sought evangelical salvation. He realized that it was very difficult for them to pursue the religious life, under the appalling conditions of destitution and disease which they suffered. He took an extraordinary interest, notwithstanding his busy campaigns, in the individual troubles of his converts. He wrote, ten years after the revival began, in 1749, a remarkable letter to Vincent Perronet, the Vicar of Shoreham (whom Charles Wesley called the Archbishop of Methodism), describing the various solutions of these difficulties as they arose. There is no document which describes so well the development of the Methodist people. It is an interesting record of the way in which John Wesley, who was constantly seeking the guidance of the Holy Spirit of God, made bold experiments of a social character. He studied medicine himself in order to deal with the diseases of the disinherited. He established a dispensary—probably the first of its kind. He formed a loan society to help the people financially distressed. Knitting Guilds and the like he organized to help poor women. These and other social experiments were quite unique at the time in the eighteenth century, and are indications of the way in which Wesley did not only passionately care for the salvation of the souls but remembered that men had bodies as well.

But perhaps the best corrective of all to the sheer individualism was his doctrine of Christian Perfection, or Entire Sanctification as it was also called. John Wesley's favourite description of it, and I think much the best, was Perfect Love. The late Dr R. W. Dale of Birmingham criticized the Methodist people for not making explicit by experiment, what was implied in Wesley's doctrine of Perfect Love. This criticism was quite valid, but the reason that the doctrine has not been more carefully examined and socially applied by the inheritors of the Wesley tradition is partly due to John Wesley himself. The doctrine as John taught it, Dr Croft Cell said, was a synthesis between the Lutheran doctrine of Justification by Faith and the Catholic Doctrine of Perfect Love. In my opinion John Wesley attempted this synthesis but failed in making it. While it is possible for a man by a single act of faith to believe in a pardoning God and to accept His forgiveness and be assured of its reality, the attempt to apply this to Entire Sanctification cannot be successful, because if a man says that he has an assurance that he is perfect, nothing is more apparent than his imperfection.

Charles Wesley, who did not accept his brother's doctrine of Instantaneous Perfection, writes:

> *Though all the precious promises*
> *I find fulfill'd in Jesu's Love,*
> *If perfect I myself profess,*
> *My own profession I disprove:*
> *The purest saint that lives below*
> *Doth his own sanctity disclaim,*
> *The wisest owns, 'I nothing know',*
> *The holiest cries, 'I nothing am!'*

Though the substance of this doctrine was Perfect Love, the Methodist people were attracted by teaching which led them to hope that they could become perfect in a moment of ecstatic experience. They met together both in the time of Wesley and afterwards and sang:

*I claim the Blessing* now.

Unfortunately they sought for a liberating emotional experience which, after moments of uplifting, frequently issued in depression.[2]

But the practice of Perfect Love, and love only becomes perfect as it is practised, was neglected by the Methodist people, because they were misled in thinking that they could achieve in a moment of ecstatic faith what can only be arrived at by disciplined practice. Perfect Love is the positive truth which would cover, and if perfect make impossible, all sins of omission, all self-indulgence. The practice of Perfect Love too must have emphasized the social character of Christian life and would have made less intolerable the social results of the Industrial Revolution, which was contemporary with the Methodist Revival; while Wesley, possibly because he had little, if any, sense of the social meaning of the Kingdom of God, did not harmonize his individual doctrine of flight from the wrath of God with his special doctrine of Perfect Love, possibly because he did not see the social significance of the Kingdom of God. The positive teaching of Christianity so necessary to our own days is really implicit in his doctrine of Perfect Love, and may become explicit in the teaching of his spiritual descendants.

### CHRISTIAN PERFECTION

The little book entitled *The Beauty of Holiness*, by Mr Baines Atkinson, especially in its early chapters which are rich in

---

[2] J. E. Rattenbury, *Conversion of the Wesleys*, pp. 193-207. *Evangelical Doctrines of Charles Wesley's Hymns*, pp. 298-319.

scriptural quotation and interpretation, is a very beautiful treatment of the subject, which I have read with great pleasure and profit. In its later chapters, Mr Atkinson defends John Wesley's doctrine of Christian Perfection, against the views which I have expressed in this and other books. At least, though my name is unmentioned, the quotations from my writings suggest this opinion. He seems to think, probably through the lack of lucidity in my writings, and judging from his numerous quotations from Holy Scripture, that I reject Faith as an essential element in sanctification. Of course I do not. My point is that the Faith exercised in Justification, which enables a man to accept the forgiveness of his sins, puts him into a new relation to God, whereas Christian Perfection postulates ethical change and cannot be achieved by such an act of faith as that which he exercised in Justification. No doubt something depends on definition of terms.

Wesley, it is true, though he used the word Christian Perfection as the title of his principal book on the subject of holiness, would not contend for the title when pressed by critics though he was ready to stand by it. I do not believe that the analogy of justification and the witness of the Spirit can be applied to Christian Perfection, nor did Charles Wesley. Any man who claims the witness of the Spirit, that he is a perfect Christian, is to my mind a deluded man.

No doubt the man who consecrates himself completely to God, will often receive a blessing such as that which Mr Atkinson the author, most simply and humbly, claims for himself. Experiences such as those which he relates do come to men often more than once in the Christian life, but do not therefore guarantee a permanent ethical change.

Wesley claimed that his doctrine was the grand depositum of Methodism; but one could wish that he had defined it with more exactness. That Mr Atkinson in his beautiful little book may be a little doubtful as to the doctrine is shown by the fact that he says: 'Wesley did not give further definition of his teaching. He did not seek to give philosophical or psychological examination of the theory. The greatest need today is not definition but that sacred impulse to claim the blessing.' I can only say that it seems a pity that Wesley's logical mind did not find an intelligible formula, for the doctrine which he asserts is the grand depositum of Methodism.

Perhaps it would be wise for all professors of Holiness to remember a saying of Fénelon: 'We are quite willing to be consumed all at once by the flames of pure love; but this rapid destruction would cost us hardly anything. It is excess of self-love which desires to be made perfect so suddenly and so cheaply.'

CHAPTER TWO

# REFLECTIONS OF AN OCTOGENARIAN

*Lo! to faith's enlightened sight,*
*All the mountain flames with light;*
*Hell is nigh, but God is nigher,*
*Circling us with hosts of fire.*

### I. EVANGELISTIC REGRESSION

ALL MY LIFE I have been deeply involved in evangelism and evangelistic appeal. My grandfather was one of the greatest of Methodist evangelistic preachers who carried on a ministry of extraordinary success for fifty years. The family tradition cherished in my home was continued in the ministerial life of my father; my goodly heritage has been a cherished possession in my own ministry. I may perhaps be pardoned for writing down after a few generalizations the impressions of seventy years, from my fourteenth year onward, of the progress or, in some ways, I must say, the regress, of evangelism in the Methodist Church.

In the early years of the nineteenth century there was little change in Methodist belief and teaching nor in the psychological atmosphere which Methodists breathed. The flame of evangelism never died out though sometimes it flickered rather dimly. The problems Wesley left behind him at his death for other people to solve dominated a period of ecclesiastical construction. There were times in the first half of the century when the difficulties of St Paul in the early Corinthian Church were repeated in Methodism. Questions of ministerial prerogatives, of lay rights, of liberty and government, created bad tempers, and sometimes expressed themselves in secessions and splits. The solvent of love, which St Paul realized was the true way of government, was often lacking. Pride, self interest, independence of spirit, and lack of humility predominated, where love might have preserved unity.

Another danger, which Wesley foresaw, was that of 'settling down on our lees'. This was often the result of the sobriety and economy of the Methodist people which led to an increase in their riches, and created, perhaps, an unconscious desire to be regarded as a respectable community.

Though evangelism never entirely died out, and the appeal for conversion was continually made, the development of an educated Ministry was not without the result of diminishing zeal for the earlier methods of field preaching and open-air appeal. Later on in the century a popular classification of ministers labled some as 'edifying' and others as 'evangelistic', and it was perhaps true that there was a tendency to forget that 'Knowledge puffeth up, but love edifieth' (buildeth up). But it must never be forgotten that the love that buildeth up in the Wesleyan tradition was not the mystical love of St John of the Cross for instance, but the practical social love of the thirteenth chapter of the First Epistle to the Corinthians, a love which in early days had expressed itself in a passion for souls, described in Charles Wesley's hymn for lay preachers in the words:

> *And love them with a zeal like Thine . . .*
> *The sheep for whom their Shepherd died.*

When the Methodist Society forgot or ignored its origin and forgot its first love—evangelism—the Primitive Methodist revival broke out, which relit the fires of early Methodism and repeated the heroic evangelism of the Wesleys, particularly in the open-air, of which their famous camp-meetings became the symbol. That revival was always characterized in my home as a rebuke of the 'worldliness' of the generation of Methodists after the death of Wesley. It was an extraordinary and richly successful revival, although its preachers were relatively illiterate men. I think it was W. T. Stead, who called the Primitive Methodist movement the first Labour Church, and the work that it did amongst the miners of Durham and the agricultural labourers of East Anglia and Wiltshire, to give conspicuous instances, had a lasting effect upon the religious and social life of England. The name 'Primitive' Methodism was justified in so far as the heroic appeals in the open-air are concerned, but in its neglect of the equally conspicuous Sacramentalism of the Wesleys and the early Methodists, the name 'Primitive' is rather misleading. But all Methodists with any sense of our distinctive mission can only thank God for the way in which these Apostolic men relit the fires of evangelism. It must be noted that the old beliefs in Hell had in no ways diminished amongst people to whom the Primitive Methodist appealed. There was nothing in the early nineteenth century which hampered a repetition of the eighteenth-century appeal.

During the middle century the most conspicuous evangelistic appeals were made by Americans. Their appeal was not so much to the outcast classes of society as to the bourgeoisie. When I was a boy at Oxford I heard D. L. Moody preach, but was too young to be impressed by his preaching. Ten years afterwards I heard him preach in Manchester and was greatly impressed by the hard-headed common sense and plain piety of his appeal. The first at least of these missions was a tremendous success, but its popular appeal was due chiefly to the hymns of Sankey. These hymns from a literary standpoint were very inferior to those of Wesley and Watts. Many of them were sentimental and silly, but the catchy tunes to which they were set captivated masses of people, and even today are popular in some quarters. I would myself regard the difference between the Wesley and Sankey hymns and the different use made of them as a distinct sign of the degeneration of the old evangelism.[1] Both in their mission and in that of successive evangelists, American and otherwise, the sentimental hymn-tune was used to create emotions not always healthy, but not ineffective.

[1] I use the word 'old evangelism', not in any sense as a repudiation of its central meaning, but as a convenient term to contrast its methods with those of a later period.

The outstanding evangelistic appeal of the nineteenth century was that of General Booth and the Salvation Army. General Booth, himself a minister of the United Methodist Church, who felt too much circumscribed by his denomination (from which he detached himself with great boldness) made his historical attack upon the outcast population of England. I well remember the sensational successes of the early days of the movement, and the many criticisms which its sensationalism, not unnaturally, created amongst quiet Church people. But there is no doubt that the movement produced not only the Salvation Army and afterwards its remarkable social developments, but awakened again in the old evangelical denominations a new spirit of evangelism.

The Welsh revival at the beginning of the twentieth century was a remarkable and almost spontaneous outburst of religious zeal. It spread like a fire through Wales, but it was unfortunately over-publicized by the new journalism. I think it might be called the last of the revivals of the old evangelism and was not affected to any extent by a loss of belief in Hell. The permanent effect of it was, I think, neutralized by the out-of-date puritanism of the Welsh sects. At the time, I recollect, I was conducting a correspondence column in a religious weekly and was informed by the members of a Welsh church that the influence of the revival was being destroyed because some of the young converts insisted on playing football. This they regarded as a great danger to their spiritual life. I informed them very frankly that if the revival was marred it would not be by the football of its converts, but by the bigotry of their critics.

Though the old evangelistic methods were employed more or less spasmodically up till 1914 and even afterwards especially in rural areas, they showed marked degeneracy in type. Certain outstanding personalities made successful appeals. The most conspicuous of them was Gipsy Smith. In his early years he preached the old-fashioned Gospel of salvation through faith in the atonement of Christ, with great effect. In his later years I knew him well; his preaching, though enormously popular, must have,

I think, been affected by the changed thought of the day. It was distinctly ethical in character, although curiously enough based on emotional appeal. He depended greatly upon his own singing of simple songs which appealed deeply to the emotions of his hearers. Gipsy Smith was a man of very remarkable natural endowments. He had the temperament of the poet, and his artistic power was of quite exceptional quality, as anyone who listened to his description of Epping Forest in spring-time must have realized. Though his reasoning was not very convincing, intuitions were. But as I have suggested, his evangelism was modified in his later days, and his influence with the unconverted masses of the people was greatly neutralized by the fact of his popularity amongst the Free Churches. His missions, supposed to appeal to the outsider, hardly in latter days reached them, because of the vast and overflowing congregations of professing Christians, who delighted in his song and speech.

Probably the years during which old evangelistic methods became antiquated were 1914-18. May I at this point recount some early personal experiences of evangelism. In my own home I inherited the traditions of the old evangelism. The Methodism of my childhood had a depth of piety which is unforgettable. I can think of nothing more unworldly than the life of my own home, or shall I say homes, since the Methodist minister of that day only stayed three years in one place. As I look back upon those early days, I am sure that my parents had no ambition, or at least showed none, for their children, except that they should be good Christians. I must admit, however, that to them to be a good Christian was to be a good Methodist. I do not think that they would have denied the possibility of other communities containing Christians, but they felt sure of Methodists and rather uncertain about anybody else. How many times as a boy did I hear statements about the superior goodness of Methodists!

The commonest was that when a notorious blackguard was dying in a village and found the ministrations of the Vicar useless he always called upon the Methodist local preacher or leader to come and talk to him about religion, as they were regarded as the real experts in the village. There undoubtedly was an almost Pharisaic complacency about the Methodists of the period. Of an earlier time I remember my grandmother telling me an illuminating incident. She showed me a pack of what were called Methodist playing-cards, which consisted of fifty-two cards, each of which had printed upon it a text of Scripture and a verse of one of Charles Wesley's hymns. When she and other Methodist girls were invited to a party (the date would be about 1820) they took no part in the games their hosts provided, but when the others were playing whist, which Methodists then regarded as a very evil thing, these Methodist maidens sat round the fire and circulated the Methodist playing-cards, which my grandmother thought to be an instance of conspicuous piety. I fear that a modern interpretation would be that anything could hardly be more objectionable than these little prigs congratulating themselves and saying what good girls they were.

The Puritanism of my home was in some ways very rigid, but I should be saying what was quite untrue if I created a feeling that the home was miserable—in point of fact, we were a happy family, very happy. Strict sabbatarianism did not annoy us: a good deal of common sense was used in its application. It may seem to modern minds ridiculous, but the distinction between Sunday and week-day games was not irrational. If on a Sunday games were played or illustrated books permitted which were not used on other days of the week, the Sunday could even be looked forward to as a day distinguished by its games and books; but in point of fact the religious services of the day occupied much of the child's time. The atmosphere of religion was quite dominant and though some expressions of self-complacency may well be criticized, the practice of genuine religion was unexceptionable. Bred in such an atmosphere the doings of the Church were the chief interest of one's life, and in my own home, largely because of our family tradition, evangelistic successes were to us thrilling news. When I was a child at school in Oxford, the first Sunday service to which I went was conducted by the newly appointed minister, none other than Hugh Price Hughes, who was to become the most famous of Methodist ministers since the time of John Wesley. He brought about a great revolution in Methodism. Though himself one of the most eminent evangelists of our denomination, even in the 1880's he had no use for the traditional doctrine of Hell. Indeed, I remember reading in one of his books, though I regret I cannot verify the quotation, a sentence something like this: 'To want to be a Christian because you are afraid of going to Hell expresses a vulgarity of mind of which I hope no member of this congregation is capable; and it is hardly less vulgar to be a Christian merely with a desire to go to Heaven.' Christianity, he said, means doing the will of God, and loving your neighbour. This struck a new note in Methodist evangelism, a social note of great significance in the days to come. To this I will return later. Though I was only ten years old at the time, the preaching of Hugh Price Hughes made me resolve to become a minister and evangelist myself and I began my career a few years later as an evangelist of the old order, though even then with some modification.

Before recording my personal experience I must write of the gradual disappearance of the doctrines of Hell Fire and of conventional ideas of heaven. Although before the nineties, in which I began my ministerial training, the teaching of F. D. Maurice and Charles Kingsley and the then famous book *Eternal Hope* of Dean Farrar had influenced the minds of many people, the doctrine of the material fire of Hell was still defended by the theological tutor at Didsbury College. Personally, the doctrine influenced me very little. It may be that when I heard about eternal fires, I felt like the Scotsman who said that he was sure that his constitution would never endure it. But discussions were frequent in my student days as to whether this fire was material or metaphorical. Later on in the nineties Dr J. A. Beet, the theological tutor of another college, made an attack upon the ancient doctrine, which caused a great sensation but expressed the feeling of many people. One remark of my father's I can never forget. He said, though he would have been the last to affirm a doctrine that he did not believe to be true, that if the bottom was knocked out of Hell, it would mean the destruction of evangelism. I have no doubt myself, that the loss of this doctrine and the loss of appeal to the fears of men, has made a profound difference to the effectiveness of the old evangelical appeals.

It is perhaps significant that I was asked years later by a man whose munificent gifts to Methodism were outstanding and who was very conservative in his theological views, why it was that ministers never preached on Hell in these days. I forget my reply, but he said: 'I should never have become a Christian if I had not been afraid of going to Hell.' Belief in a God who tortured people became impossible to everyone. Even Roman Catholics, who still teach a doctrine of Hell, have not been unaffected in this matter. One of their most famous theologians told me that, though the Church retained the doctrine of Hell, in his own fraternity it was often discussed whether anyone ever went there. Some of his brethren he said even had hopes of the final salvation of Judas Iscariot.

Though I would not assert that the decay of evangelical appeal is altogether explained by the loss of the doctrine of Hell Fire, it seems foolish not to realize the change that the alteration in belief has made in the psychological atmosphere of our time. In the loss of this belief, the danger of forgetfulness of the judgements of God can too easily be ignored.

In my early ministry in Leicester, Nottingham, and London up till 1918, there were many responses to the evangelical appeal for which I can only be grateful. After the First World War a marked difference in the thinking of the people to whom I had to speak could not but be discerned. For one thing, the men who had experienced a real hell in the trenches of France, could not imagine anything worse in any possible future, and other influences were working in the popular mind. The scientific discoveries and theories which had been discussed for half a century amongst the intellectuals had filtered slowly into the minds of the people who, for many years, had been untouched by them. The effect of biblical criticism which had become helpful to the understanding of the Bible by students seemed to the general public destructive of its truth. Nor must it be forgotten that in the days between the two wars problems of unemployment and the like overshadowed the daily life of great multitudes. Also the Communist propaganda, though not appealing so deeply to the British as to other European populations, offered attractions more immediately appealing to people living in distressful conditions than those offered by the Christian pulpit.

CHAPTER THREE

# REFLECTIONS OF AN OCTOGENARIAN

*All are not lost or wandered back;*
  *All have not left Thy Church and Thee;*
*There are who suffer for Thy sake,*
  *Enjoy Thy glorious infamy,*
  *Esteem the scandal of the Cross;*
*And only seek divine applause.*

*See how great a flame aspires,*
  *Kindled by a spark of grace!*
*Jesu's love the nations fires,*
  *Sets the kingdoms on a blaze.*
*To bring fire on earth He came;*
  *Kindled in some hearts it is:*
*O that all might catch the flame,*
  *All partake the glorious bliss!*

## II. A METHODIST REVIVAL WITH A NEW NOTE

THE OUTSTANDING event of the last decades of the nineteenth century in Methodism was the revolution brought about by the personality and mission of Hugh Price Hughes. He it was who broke down the walls of the enclosed garden of traditional Methodism. I would not say that in breaking down the walls he did not destroy some fragrant flowers of traditional piety—no reform is ever accomplished entirely without loss—but he opened out to the Denomination wide vistas when its garden walls were destroyed. The Forward Movement was the name he gave to his campaign—the name has often been used since to describe other campaigns by other people. The movement was expounded week by week in a journal, which he started and edited brilliantly—*The Methodist Times*. Week by week the cannonades of the journal against ancient Methodist customs and traditions startled and shocked good old-fashioned people, but inspired with hope the new generation. The journal often spoke of the grip of the dead hand upon the Methodism of the day, and how often occurred (sometimes when speaking of the Ministry cabined and confined by customs no longer of practical benefit) the phrase, 'Loose him and let him go'; Hugh Price Hughes was successful in bringing about this emancipation.

A number of new and popular attacks were made on the outside world, in great centres of population, London, Manchester, Leeds and Birmingham in particular. In the provincial centres especially, huge Chapels once crowded with people which had become empty were sometimes demolished and in their place were built popular Central Halls. Others were entirely transformed and reseated to make them suitable places of gathering and worship for the artisan population.

But London was the centre of the activity of Hugh Price Hughes himself. He hired for Sunday services what then was the most popular concert hall in London, St James's, Piccadilly. Here he introduced an orchestral concert before his service began, and the music of the service itself was rendered by a competent brass band. These innovations shocked the inheritors of the earlier Puritanism. C. H. Spurgeon sent Mr Price Hughes an indignant letter of criticism of such methods. While the evening service at St James's Hall was an evangelistic service in which the thunderous appeal of Hugh Price Hughes to people 'to here and now submit yourselves to Christ' (his favourite phrase) was responded to by thousands of people, the most distinctive feature of the new venture was his so-called Conference on Sunday afternoons, in which he outlined all sorts of social reforms. In earlier days, though the Primitive Methodist Society had at least in some places engaged in political activities in the interests of the labouring people of which it was largely composed, the main Wesleyan body—'t'owd body' as the Yorkshire people called it, was largely Conservative. Memorable passages will come to mind in the novels of Disraeli where Wesleyan support for Conservatism is especially noted. But it was not because they were political that the Wesleyans were

Conservative, but because they were non-political, and felt that they had to do with the World to come, rather than this world; the consequences of the piety being that they did not want things as they were to be disturbed. I well remember, for instance, at a rather later date, how a conspicuous Methodist business man was asked to stand for Parliament, and after some thought refused because it would be inconvenient, if not impossible, for him to get back to his own locality on Sundays in those days of more difficult travelling, to carry on as a local preacher and the reader of a men's Bible class. This is a fair type of the Wesleyan attitude before the Hugh Price Hughes revolution. And this traditional attitude of Wesleyan Methodism was one against which Mr Hughes violently fulminated.

Hugh Price Hughes, however, preached the necessity of political action by Christians both local and national. Not to vote was a sin according to Mr Hughes, whereas many early Methodists had regarded it as a virtue. In the strongest language he denounced the traditional pietism of his Denomination, and formulated practical programmes of social and political attack. The addresses which he delivered at his Sunday afternoon Conferences had a great influence upon the young publicists of the day. David Lloyd George for instance told me, and I think said more than once in public, that nothing influenced his own political outlook more than these Conferences of Hugh Price Hughes. Lloyd George spoke of him as the greatest Welshman who had ever lived.

It was not only in the political sphere that an entire change of attitude was brought about by the Forward Movement, but also in the denominational. The older Methodists frequently repudiated the title of Nonconformists. They felt themselves really to be Anglicans who had been badly treated by the Anglican authorities. Not till 1897 did they call themselves a Church, but always a Society. They treasured and used the liturgies of the Church of England, which even to this day are used at least for Holy Communion everywhere, and for Morning Prayer in many churches. Hugh Price Hughes, though himself a High

Sacramentalist and a lover of the liturgies of the Church of England, whereas he disliked the title of Dissenter, realized the obvious facts of separation, but always insisted on calling Methodists and indeed other Nonconformists 'Free Churchmen'. He was one of the organizers and perhaps the chief initiator of the Free Church Council wherein Methodists joined the other Evangelical Free Churches in a fellowship which was quite novel to them. The Evangelical Free Church Council in its earlier years brought about a fraternization of the Free Churches with each other which gave them a new unity—a unity largely of social enthusiasm. Generally speaking, the Free Church Council was best known in the political field, and indeed greatly strengthened the Liberal Party and no doubt had a great share in the Liberal victory of 1906. In some ways this may have been unfortunate, but its early political activities were undoubtedly inspired by moral and social problems. Their social and political enthusiasm, however, gave an impression to the public that the Council was merely an organization of a political party though masquerading as an ecclesiastical body.

The new unity of the Free Churches was by no means the only expression of the desire of Hugh Price Hughes for ecclesiastical union. He was associated with his one-time colleague, Doctor (afterwards Sir) Henry Lunn in the formation of the Grindelwald Conferences which brought together Anglicans and Free Churchmen in social intercourse perhaps for the first time, and unquestionably the movement for union amongst the Churches of our day owes not a little to these Conferences. The principal instrument of the activity of Hugh Price Hughes (the West London Mission) broke down not only the political and denominational traditions of the Methodists but some of its constitutional regulations. Though authorized by the Methodist Conference its novel organization made great breaches in normal Methodist government. The halls and houses which it used were either hired, or, if they became the property of the mission, not placed upon the Model Deed. When Hugh Price Hughes said 'Loose him and let him go' and the Conference consented in his case, he liberated himself from the normal local financial control of a Methodist Circuit, and from other things which would have impeded his course.

A great innovation was the creation under the superintendency of Mrs Hugh Price Hughes of the West London Mission Sisterhood, which was greatly criticized at the time as being a Romanish institution. The Sisterhood was composed of a number of ladies of culture, who for the most part gave their services voluntarily. They could find no ordinary occupational or professional sphere in the England of seventy years ago, so they devoted their lives to social services, and were pioneers in many spheres of women's work. The initial experiments in many social services now taken over by the Welfare State were made by the early efforts of this remarkable body of women, several of whom have distinguished themselves in the life of the country.

These changes of outlook and work which expressed the dynamic personality of Hugh Price Hughes, were first met with great criticism and suspicion in many quarters, but entirely altered the outlook of the Methodist people. Hugh Price Hughes was often regarded as a great Puritan, and indeed in the political sphere, especially in his denunciation of Parnell as an immoral man and therefore unfit for parliamentary government, he stood for a Puritanism which menaced the statesmanship of the time and influenced the action of the Government. That great journalist W. T. Stead called him 'A judgement day in Trousers', and yet 'Puritan' is a very misleading and indeed bad description of the gaiety and joyfulness of his life and religion. In theology I should claim he was definitely anti-puritan; he had no use for a mere negative religion and did not admire a life which was a catalogue of abstinences. He did not think of our Lord merely as sinless, but chiefly as the Light of the World, who by the radiance and beauty of his character illumined everything that he touched. This undoubtedly was not the puritan conception, but rather that of F. D. Maurice and Kingsley, and of the contemporary theology of the Incarnation. It is important to note that with all his social, political, and journalistic activities Hugh Price Hughes was primarily an enthusiastic Evangelist whose favourite quotation was, as he called it, the immortal epigram of Horace Bushnell: 'The soul of all improvement is the improvement of the soul.'

Though one rightly thinks of Hugh Price Hughes as the central figure of this Methodist revolution, his keen, enthusiastic spirit inspired innovations throughout the whole country. The first group of Central Halls which were built or the great public halls hired, in London, Manchester, Birmingham, and Edinburgh, were followed afterwards by the erection of many others, through the munificent generosity of Mr Joseph Rank, the value of whose gifts can hardly be over-estimated. The creation of these Central Halls was one of the notable facts in the Christian life of England in the later decades of the nineteenth century and the first two of the twentieth. The result of the appeal made through them to the working people of this country was amazingly successful. Many thousands of people thronged them every Sunday. The principal Missions of this character were built upon sensational conversions of notorious evil doers.

Most, if not all, of these Missions gave special attention to a large variety of social organizations. The most striking and fruitful were the work of S. F. Collier, whose organizing genius found expression in all kinds of social experiments of the highest value, through the Manchester Mission of which he was the superintendent. Though there were instances of failure as well as success before 1914, it was after the first great World War that their effectiveness diminished. Since the first war the gradual development of the Welfare State has made some of these social organizations redundant, but it must never be forgotten that the great sums of money spent on central halls and the powerful appeal they made to thousands of people, chiefly of the artisan class, through their evangelical message and their social organizations, were of great national benefit which, I think, has not been recognized as it should have been. The Central Hall movement in itself was an evangelical revival of a remarkable character, with a new role of social service.

The Forward Movement expressed itself in a variety of social and semi-political activities. To catalogue them is unnecessary, but the topics discussed at the St James's Hall Conference on Sunday afternoons by Mr Price Hughes were followed by a variety of campaigns. In the Methodist denominations new inspirations were given to Movements such as Temperance, the Emancipation of Women, and various forms of rescue work, and peace organizations. Problems and questions familiar to us in these days were unfamiliar in Methodist quarters seventy years ago, but the Christian obligation to make the world a better world was stressed with an entirely new emphasis. The chief concern of Hugh Price Hughes was the life of London. Often he pleaded, as did Savonarola for Florence, that Christ would make London the City of God.

The results of the Forward Movement were by no means exclusively denominational. The Methodists made their contribution to the silent and almost unobserved social revolution of England. The old Evangelical, although an individualist, never lacked in social service. The words of Charles Wesley expressed both their ideal and practice:

> *To serve the present age,*
> *My calling to fulfil:*
> *O may it all my powers engage*
> *To do my Master's will!*

The many charities and philanthropies that had their origin in Evangelical conviction bear witness to a sense of the obligation of human service. Everything that could be done to relieve poverty and misery and unhappiness was done by them and no greater example of social service, and of ingenious social service, is to be found than in the practice of John Wesley. How could it be otherwise with men whose ideal was perfect love? And yet, while works of pity and charity were universal among Evangelicals, they do seem to have taken poverty as an irremovable evil. They misunderstood and misapplied the words often quoted: 'The poor ye have always with you.' Though they relieved poverty, they had little sense of any obligation to undermine it. They failed (this is even true, as we have seen, of John Wesley) to realize some of the implications of the Kingdom of Christ on earth.[1] It never seemed to occur to them that it was difficult to teach people (those who lived under conditions such as those brought about through the Industrial Revolution in this country) not to worry about the future. The social activities and teaching of Hugh Price Hughes entirely altered their outlook. Earlier Methodists had considered politics as a very doubtful pursuit for men whose first duty was to seek the Kingdom of God. Hugh Price Hughes taught that it was wicked not to vote at an election and shocked many people in consequence.

Perhaps I may write, for what it is worth, my impression of movements in which I have personally participated and on which I have long reflected. But this is a personal reflection of an octogenarian and must not be thought of as an historical document. Methodism, I think, made no contribution to the new social Christian ideology of which the Forward Movement was an expression. Indeed, the first Christian revolts against the economic beliefs of the time came from writers like Thomas Carlyle and John Ruskin, and perhaps it may be especially claimed that Ruskin's *Unto this Last* was the first and perhaps the most influential of all Christian criticisms of the hard and heathen economic views of the Christians of the day. But there was a definite—I will not say 'change'—but deepening in social theology which is chiefly traceable to that great nineteenth-century prophet, F. D. Maurice. He was not a writer for the people, but his disciple, Charles Kingsley, felt it his mission in life to popularize his teaching. One of the most influential books of the time was Kingsley's *Alton Lock*, which, supplemented by a variety of pamphlets from his pen, made very plain what was obscure in Maurice. In his autobiography,[2] Mr G. W. E. Russell gives a valuable account of the influence of these writers.

Practical steps to implement the new social teaching are seen

[1] See pp. 15-16.   [2] *Fifteen Chapters of Autobiography* (see Chapter 14).

in the Guild of St Matthew founded by the Rev. Stuart Headlam in 1877. This was the precursor of the Christian Social Union of which the saintly theologian, Dr Westcott, became the first President. His teaching, too, was somewhat obscure. Canon Liddon is credited at least with one jest when he accounted for a London fog by saying that it was caused by Canon Westcott opening his study window in Amen Court! But the influence of his incarnational theology was very deep and more popular expositions followed in the writing and speaking of Dr Scott Holland and Bishop Gore. But the purpose of these distinguished thinkers and writers was not so much to catch the popular ear as to influence the clergy and awaken the slumbering conscience of the Church of England. Their teaching soon found practical expressions in the University and Public School Settlements established in the London slums. The bringing together of the privileged and unprivileged classes was of great value. The work these institutions did was largely educational. But something perhaps was wanted in dealing with the masses of the English people which these institutions did not quite supply. It is true that in localities, heroic workers like Father Dolling and Father Stanton made great popular appeal of a local character but the appeal to the artisan as such needed a dynamic which was, I think, supplied by the great Methodist appeal to the working people of England.

The dynamic personality of Hugh Price Hughes, his weekly journal, his social innovations and his stirring appeals and political influence already referred to in no small measure gave the theology of Maurice and Westcott by which he had been greatly influenced the popular appeal that they had lacked. Also the positive evangelical note of the Methodist tradition was one which gave warmth to the valuable social propaganda of the Christian Social Union.

No feature in the religious life of England at the turn of the century, as I have already noted, was more important than the building of the great Central Halls of Methodism in the principal centres of population. Many of these structures were magnificent buildings, well placed in central positions, which made a definite appeal to the artisans of England. The fact that many thousands of people were gathered together in these halls and great hired buildings on a Sunday was a notable phenomenon. It is quite certain that no such effective appeal was being made elsewhere to the British working men. But in addition to their evangelism these buildings were networks of social organizations of every sort imaginable.

The difference between British and Continental Socialism has often been noted. Whereas on the Continent the movements have usually been atheistic and the motives of envy and hatred strongly appealed to, such motives have not been commonly conspicuous or dominant in England—the truth being that many of the propagandists have been Christian people seeking the betterment of their fellow countrymen for no other reason than their desire to obey the commandments of Jesus to build up His Kingdom on earth.

Though I am sure the contribution both of thought and practice of organizations like the Christian Social Union has been of the utmost importance, the Methodist dynamic and its power of reaching the people from the level of the people is a factor that cannot be ignored. It must not be forgotten that the early development of the political Labour Party was largely contemporaneous with the Methodist Forward Movement. The fact that many of its leaders were Methodist local preachers counted for much more than people realized. Mr Sidney Webb's tribute to the activity of Primitive Methodism amongst the Durham miners is well known, but the wider influence of the Methodist local preacher, often himself an artisan, has perhaps been less stressed. Possibly the ablest organizer of the Labour Party as it exists today was Mr Arthur Henderson, a Methodist local preacher who, even when he became Foreign Secretary, said in my hearing that he was proud to say he was a local preacher. There were many like him, men who carried the enthusiasm of Methodism into the early Labour movement. People who attended Labour meetings as I did at the beginning of this century were surprised at their almost apocalyptic enthusiasm. They often were possessed with the spirit of a Methodist revival meeting. Indeed, some of the leading Labour statesmen of our own day have expressed deep regret that that spirit seems now to be lacking in their Party.

It must not be assumed, however, that the social teaching and programmes of Hugh Price Hughes were accepted by all Methodist people. On the contrary, many enthusiastic men were frozen out of the *bourgeois* churches of the Methodist middle classes. But for my part I cannot but be thankful that the definitely Christian element permeated as much as it did the struggles for better conditions of the English people.

I do not doubt that there were defects or at least dangers in the social emphasis of the Forward Movement. Sometimes the social ideal lost its connexion with evangelical life and degenerated into mere humanism, but one thing is clear: the sense of social obligation and the sensitiveness of the social conscience have saved Methodists from a mere other-worldly individualism. The truth is that the synthesis between individual and social religion has been insufficiently realized and expressed. It is necessary for us to realize that the Gospel of the Kingdom which Jesus taught is one with the gospel of personal salvation which evangelicals derive, as did the Reformers, from the teachings of St Paul. These are not exclusive gospels. Looking back upon the social enthusiasms of half a century ago, I feel that the new note in the Evangelical gospel may be regarded as a trumpet call to our own days. Then, we knew the droppings of a shower, but the shower is yet to come, and nothing matters more than the realization and formulation as a doctrine of the one Gospel of the New Testament in its two-fold individual and social expressions, as I shall try to show, however imperfectly, in the final chapters of this book.

CHAPTER FOUR

# REFLECTIONS OF AN OCTOGENARIAN

*By Thine unerring Spirit led,*
  *We shall not in the desert stray;*
*We shall not full direction need,*
  *Nor miss our providential way;*
*As far from danger as from fear,*
*While love, almighty love, is near.*

### III. THE EXPERIENCES OF AN EVANGELIST

As I was intimately associated with the Evangelical Movement of which I have been writing, it is perhaps fitting that in my octogenarian reflections I should give some account of my personal activity. I was the ministerial founder in 1902 of the Nottingham Albert Hall Mission. This I think was the last of the first group of great central missions. Afterwards in 1907, four years after the death of Hugh Price Hughes, I succeeded to the superintendency of the West London Mission, where I worked for eighteen years until my health broke down. I would like to record an impression of earlier work of the same sort that I did in Leicester where I had my first contact with working-class communities. In 1897 I took charge of a Mission which was conducted in school premises in an artisan area. The successful work required much larger premises to accommodate the people we were dealing with and a large hall seating 1,100 people was built, opened, and crowded largely with young men and women of the neighbourhood. I came into contact with a number of young men who had been influenced by a secularist teacher of the name of Gould, a man whom I never met, but for whose character and teaching I have the highest admiration. A considerable number of these young men responded to our evangelical appeal and joined our Church. They told Mr Gould of what had happened and to my surprise and joy, instead of criticizing my evangelism, he told them that I might do them more good than he could do. I never came across a group of people more eager to learn. On a Saturday afternoon for instance they sacrificed their sports and met with me to read Ruskin's *Unto this Last* and Carlyle's *Past and Present* and similar books. One of them, a lad of sixteen, suddenly recited to me one day a poem of Robert Browning's and I found out that he had taken the two well-known volumes of *Selections of Browning's Poems*, dismembered them, and fastened them page by page on the loom at which he was working, and had actually committed the two volumes to memory! A man somewhat older, who had been an unbeliever in Christianity, told us one day in a public meeting that he was first attracted to Jesus Christ by reading a book which he called 'I-per-ty-ar'—a book the name of which I did not recognize until he spoke of its substance, when to my surprise it proved to be Charles Kingsley's *Hypatia*. That a working man of no education should have heard the voice of Christ in this strikingly philosophical novel was another sign of the intellectual activities of these Leicester artisans. From contact with them and their Socialist enthusiasms they were also disciples of Robert Blatchford and his *Merrie England*. I learnt much most valuable to me in after years.

The largest public hall in Nottingham, the Albert Hall, had been bought by a group of enthusiastic Methodists and I was appointed to organize a mission centre there. There was a general opinion at that time that if a hall or theatre or any conspicuous public building was taken and used for religious services the public would crowd to it. Perhaps when such services were a novelty this was true. But when I began my work the novelty was wearing bare, and although the services were widely advertised only a few hundred people came to a hall accommodating two thousand, and they were obviously from various Nonconformist chapels. My experience of the appeal of Christian Socialism to the young men of Leicester, and my personal indignation that Christian people had done so little to ameliorate appalling social conditions made me resolve to preach on the application of Christianity to the social life of the people. My advertisement of the six social sermons I proposed to preach increased the numbers of the congregation, but by no means filled the hall. Then an extraordinary thing happened. In an excited moment I was guilty of what I should think now an intemperate expression of speech and said to my rather complacent-looking audience: 'Lay down your New Testament and read the *Clarion.*' The *Clarion* was then the chief organ of Socialism in this country and though afterwards Robert Blatchford, its editor, became an opponent of Christianity, at the time when I made this rather foolish request there was no sign of what afterwards happened. The sentence I have quoted gained a great publicity, and was quoted in a good many newspapers with the implication that a Christian minister had repudiated the New Testament and taken to the *Clarion.* It may seem a strange result, but my quite impromptu indiscretion was followed next Sunday by a crowd of people which packed the hall to overflowing and which continued till the hall was burnt down several years later.

Though this gave me the ear of many people it did not result in much visible spiritual fruit—indeed one could hardly have expected that it would. In the following January, however, there broke out an extraordinary response to the evangelical appeal. The most notorious woman in Nottingham, who had been imprisoned thirty times, became converted at one of the services. At the time she was living with a man of similar character who happened to be absent from Nottingham when her conversion took place. When at his return, through the care of some devout old people, he was brought to one of the services he himself experienced evangelical conversion, and incidentally became a Christian man for whom I had the greatest respect. It was a joy to me to conduct the marriage of these two people.

Afterwards there followed a series of remarkable demonstrations of the power of the spirit of God, and a number of people (a blatant atheist, disreputable and vicious persons among them) became reformed characters and joined our Church. Personally I hardly like to recount these incidents, but did at the time feel that I was not responsible for what happened. The conviction that I had then of the actual working of the finger of God amongst these people has never left me, but in times of doubt and depression the experience of those days has been an indescribable encouragement. With the help of several Sisters, all kinds of social activities were developed and the Mission which then was started has continued, centred at the new Albert Hall built on the ashes of the old one, successful to this day. Before the new hall was built, however, I was sent by the Methodist Conference to the West London Mission which, after the death of Hugh Price Hughes, had fallen on difficult times. St James's Hall, the centre of this work, was sold and on its site the Piccadilly Hotel was built. The Mission could find no other suitable public hall for its services, and notwithstanding the heroic work of my predecessor, C. Ensor Walters, it was rapidly disintegrating and only saved by the continuing social work of the Sisterhood of some twenty to thirty devoted women. When I took over the work the Sunday services were held in a renovated Chapel in Great Queen Street. It was a great stroke of good fortune, perhaps I ought to say Providence, that this building, unsuitable for the work, was condemned as unfit by the London County Council. In consequence it was demolished and on its site was built the Kingsway Hall and its adjacent Mission premises. During the four years of reconstruction of buildings I held services on Sundays in the Lyceum Theatre, which still was associated in the mind of the people with Henry Irving and Ellen Terry. By means of these services it became possible to rebuild the Mission. The congregation, numbering at least 3,000 every Sunday evening, was extraordinarily mixed in character. It is no exaggeration to say that people of all classes attended it, and several times the Austrian and Russian Embassies asked for boxes in the theatre which we were glad to allot to them. The response to the evangelical appeal was constant and though the whole congregation could not get into Kingsway Hall when we re-opened it most of it could, though for a time we were compelled to hold overflow services in the mission premises.

Important and useful as these services were, the social work of the sisterhood under the devoted and able guidance of Mrs Price Hughes was not less, perhaps in some ways, more, important. Without detailing its many and varied activities, I would like to make some reference to its rescue work. Sisters could be found every night of the week from ten o'clock till two o'clock in the morning near Piccadilly Circus striving to rescue prostitutes. One of them, Sister Mildred, lived in a flat near Leicester Square, the rent of which was paid by Mr Hall Caine the novelist, who took a great interest in the work. Sister Mildred was always at home to any woman, however disreputable, who came to see her—and many came. Sisters whom I did not personally know, who had left the Mission before I came to it, had been wonderfully successful. Two of them especially spoke to the disreputable and often despairing girls whom they found on the streets, telling them of the love of Jesus and assuring them that if they repented of their sins and trusted in Him they would find salvation. I mention this appeal because on the visit I paid to Canada in 1911 I met, or heard of, five prostitutes rescued from the streets of London who were living clean and respectable lives. One of them, who came to speak to me after a service I conducted in a great Presbyterian church in Toronto, told me the story of her conversion, and the minister of the Church told me that she was one of his most valued workers.

I would not have it thought, however, that this evangelistic appeal was the only thing that was done for these women; we had as well rescue homes which were successful in housing and helping them. The Rescue Work, with Rescue Homes, was carefully organized and rich in good results, and varied as the conditions during the last seventy years required varying treatment. The record of the mission in this work has been one for which the Methodist Church may be thankful.

After the great war a change took place in what I may call

the psychological atmosphere. Though it would be untrue to say that there was no response to the evangelical appeal, the attitude of people to the Gospel suffered considerable change. In my early evangelical career I found that people were really grieved that they had sinned against God and pleaded for His forgiveness. The experience of the psalmist, 'Against Thee only have I sinned', was frequent enough then, but decreasingly frequent as the years went on. I remember well a sailor who, when he arrived at a London port, spent all the money he had saved in the foulest drunkenness and debauchery. He came to me one night, crushed and broken with disgust at his own beastliness, anxious to live a better life; but when I began to talk to him about God, it was just vagueness to him. The feeling that he was a beast and not a man was strong enough, but that he had offended in any way a just and merciful Father was quite meaningless to him. This was quite different from my earlier experiences of people of a similar character. As I said earlier, the absence of a fear of Hell and Judgement counted, I am sure, to a great extent for this change of outlook, but that was by no means the only thing that counted.

While I do not suppose that soldiers in the trenches were much concerned with the new psychology, it was not without its effect on the minds of preachers and others. In my Nottingham days when Robert Blatchford made his famous attack on Christianity, I participated in the controversy and as an evidence of the reality of Christianity quoted instances of conversion at Nottingham, such as those I have related. A member of the *Clarion* staff whom I afterwards came to know, told me that he was present at an editorial meeting of the journal which discussed the religious controversy with which its columns were filled, when Robert Blatchford said that he found these instances of conversion the most difficult argument of Christianity to meet. I have often wondered what he would have said if he had known some of the later psychological writings. They certainly influenced the minds of many people, who because there was a more accurate analysis of the mental processes by which conversion was brought about, tended to forget that the analysis of the process does not explain the power that works through it.

As I add my own experiences to those of others and reflect upon the evangelism and the evangelistic methods of the last seventy years, my conviction of the truth of the old Gospel message of salvation for individuals has not in the least changed. At the same time I realize that other methods than those we used must be found to make contact with the individuals who really need the Gospel of Christ. It is no use cleaving to old methods because they were effective in the past. The weapons of Chivalry used by that strange idealist Don Quixote should make us all realize that new instruments are needed for new situations. I have felt it to be rather a pitiful thing to watch the gradual degeneration and decay of old evangelistic methods. For instance, in rural areas, it was the common practice in Methodist village chapels to hold what they called Revival Missions, often annually; when they were a novelty they had a great value in villages. I myself have come across men who in their youth were dissolute persons but were converted at these missions and became genuine Christian men. Such missions rarely take place today. I think the reason is that they deteriorated in character. In some degenerate forms they seem to be modelled on Music Hall entertainments, the substance of which were sentimental ditties of a more or less religious character, and occasionally, though perhaps rarely, comic elements were not lacking. But the demand for them amongst sensible people rapidly declined. The unfortunate thing is, that in rural areas, and I think of one which I know very well, while the families of the Methodist farmers retain their allegiance to the village chapel no effort is being made to reach the village loafers to whom the appeal of the old missioner was often quite effective. The loss of evangelistic zeal in some of these churches is not easy to account for. In another chapter I shall deal more carefully with the modern situation as I see it, and with causes both in the world and the Church which have apparently cooled down the evangelical fervour of past days. But while I express my belief in the old Gospel—the evangelical interpretation by the Wesleys of the Pauline Gospel—it is not less of it that I want, but more. Along with the individual appeal of the Pauline Gospel we need better to realize the collective good news which Jesus announced —'The Kingdom of God has arrived'—and before I deal with the modern situation I will try to examine the meaning of the Gospel of Jesus.

I have ventured to write down these autobiographical reminiscences and reflections as an introduction to the doctrine of the twofold Gospel because I write not only as a biblical student but as a practical evangelist.

PART TWO

THE TWOFOLD GOSPEL

THE KINGDOM AND THE CHURCH

CHAPTER FIVE

# THE GOOD NEWS

*Hark the glad sound! the Saviour comes,*
*The Saviour promised long;*
*Let every heart prepare a throne,*
*And every voice a song.*

*He comes the broken heart to bind,*
*The bleeding soul to cure,*
*And with the treasures of His grace*
*To enrich the humble poor.*

ACCORDING to St Mark, Jesus commenced His mission by saying: 'The time is fulfilled, and the Kingdom of God is at hand, repent ye and believe the gospel.' These words may perhaps be paraphrased thus: 'Change your mind, believe the good news that the Kingdom of God has come.' The words 'has come' or 'has arrived' or 'is here' are expressions which Dr C. H. Dodd confidently asserts are the true translations of the original words.

His conclusion is based on a careful examination of the two Greek words translated in the English Bible as 'at hand' or 'arrived' and proof of their identity of meaning is to be found in his book, *The Parables of the Kingdom*.[1] The Kingdom of God, an irruption of eschatological power into this world,[2] which is

---

[1] pp. 42-6.

[2] More detailed notes on certain modern interpretations of apocalyptic and eschatology appear elsewhere but a note on the simple meaning of the words may be helpful to some readers. Apocalyptic is a term applied to a special style of Jewish religious writing concerning the purposes of God in history. This writing was born in times of crisis, and its language is often highly coloured, violent, and symbolical. Its authors claim for it that it is a direct revelation of the message of God by way of dreams and visions. Eschatology is a term which is in increasing use in modern theological discussion, and in the hands of various

God's action without any human assistance, as Professor Bultmann writes—'The powers of the world to come'—according to Dr Dodd actually took place. Earth was invaded by heaven. The eternal order broke into the world of time and space. This he has described as Realized Eschatology. If this claim of Dr Dodd is true, and his verbal argument seems to be quite conclusive, the results have far-reaching effects. Much in the following pages is based on the acceptance of the fact of 'Realized Eschatology'.

'Believe the Gospel', says St Mark, that is, believe the good news. The words of Jesus simply mean that the Kingdom of God has arrived and this is good news. The word 'Gospel', as used by Jesus here, lacks the technical meaning which afterwards it came to have (when its implications were realized). It is good news. When the prophets of Israel spoke of the coming of God to earth, they spoke of catastrophic judgements. In the centuries just preceding the coming of Christ, and in Christ's own time, and even afterwards, many writings which are now generally called Apocalyptic were circulated amongst the Jews and greatly influenced the minds of the contemporaries of Jesus. A general expectation of the breaking in to the world of divine power, awful judgements, and catastrophic cosmic events was common. John the Baptist evidently looked for their immediate coming and warned people to prepare for the dreadful day of judgement of unquenchable fire and terror, then were solemnly warned by him to flee from the wrath to come. But when Jesus said 'believe the good news' that the Kingdom of God has arrived, He spoke not of the coming of God in judgement but of His coming in mercy. His good news was joyful news and so

authors acquires a variety of shades of meaning. In general, however, it may be said that it is the study of all those problems which arise from the consideration of God's final purpose in history. It deals with 'the last things', but also with the process by which this final consummation is reached. Sometimes it is used very loosely merely to describe ends rather than means, but properly it treats of the order which is beyond time and space and of the consummation of all things.

**(See also 'Additional Note'**, p. 143, *infra*.)

surprising that John the Baptist wondered whether He was really the man sent from heaven, 'the son of man' whom the Apocalyptists expected to come to judgement. John's doubts are expressed by the question of his messengers to Jesus: 'Art thou he that should come or look we for another.'[3] 'Jesus answered and said unto them, Go and shew John again those things which ye do hear and see: the blind receive their sight, and the lame walk, the lepers are cleansed, and the deaf hear, the dead are raised up, and the poor have the gospel preached to them. And blessed is he, whosoever shall not be offended in me.'

Jesus claimed that the finger of God was at work in these deeds. These deeds of mercy fulfilled in actual practice the claim that Jesus made at Nazareth of Messiahship:
'The Spirit of the Lord is upon me,
*Because* he hath anointed me to preach the gospel to the poor;
He hath sent me to heal the brokenhearted, to preach deliverance to the captives,
And recovering of sight to the blind,
To set at liberty them that are bruised,
To preach the acceptable year of the Lord.'[4]

In my paraphrase of the words of Jesus it will be noticed that instead of 'repent' I write 'change your mind'. The Greek word '*metanoia*', translated 'repentance' in the New Testament, seems really to have a wider meaning. Derivatively the word means 'change of mind'. In any review of a man's past this, no doubt, would involve sorrow and regret for sin, but what Jesus asks for as He announces the good news of the Kingdom of God on earth, which we shall see is a statement of the deepest revolutionary character, is an entirely changed attitude of mind and outlook.

Another problem is the meaning of the word 'Kingdom'. The Hebrew word '*Malkuth*', which is translated in the Septuagint and the New Testament by the Greek word '*Basileia*',

[3] Matthew 11:3.    [4] Luke 4:18-19.

always means—authorities tell us—the rule or reign of God. But the Greek word is more ambiguous and can be translated either 'reign' or 'realm'. In point of fact, Dr Moffatt more often translates it in the New Testament 'realm'. Scholars often warn us not to confuse the word 'kingdom' with our use of it as an area over which a king rules. They emphasize the fact that the main idea of the word is 'rulership'. But whatever lexical interpretation is given to the word it is impossible to think of 'rulership' without a corresponding area or community to be ruled over. When the Lord's Prayer says, 'Thy kingdom come. Thy will be done in earth as it is in heaven', it does define a sphere—heaven—which is the realm of God, and another—earth—which we pray may become His realm, where, we pray, His will may be done.

What John expected, and what seems to have been generally expected even later, was a manifestation of the divine power of one who will come into the world whetting his glittering sword, with the majesty and pomp of oriental grandeur. When God's kingdom actually did come it was an expression of something infinitely greater than oriental grandeur—'love came down at Christmas'. The coming of God's kingdom, with and through Jesus, was simply the attack on the world, may one say, of divine love—'the Son of man came to seek and to save that which was lost'. At the end of the first century, after men had had time to reflect on the many sayings of Jesus which they had but dimly understood while he was here, the Fourth Gospel sums up the coming of the Kingdom and the King in the great words: 'God so loved the world, that he gave his only begotten Son... God sent not his Son into the world to condemn the world; but that the world through him might be saved.'

The coming of the Kingdom and the King formed a new epoch in the history of mankind. This is clearly expressed by Jesus in the contrast between the times of John the Baptist and His own.[5] John the Baptist—the last of the Hebrew prophets—was the forerunner of the new epoch. Like the prophets before

[5] cf. Matthew 11[7-91].

Him, he viewed the coming Kingdom of God from a distance. The view he had may be compared with the view of the promised land given to Moses though he was not permitted to enter into it. A little one, said Jesus, in the Kingdom of God is greater than John the Baptist. Jesus initiated a new epoch when he announced that the Kingdom of God had come. It seems strange to think of John the Baptist outside the Kingdom of God. There is a sense, of course, in which this is not true, but it is quite plain that there is a sense in which it is, and what that is we must now consider.

> *I found God there, His visible Power;*
> *Yet felt in my heart, amid all its sense,*
> *Of that Power, an equal evidence,*
> *That His love, there too, was the nobler dower.*
> *For the loving worm within its, clod,*
> *Were diviner than a loveless god*
> *amid his worlds I will dare to say.*

Though these words of Robert Browning apply to a different situation they may well be read in relation to the coming of the Kingdom of God. The common expectation was that this would be an irruption of the Divine Glory, staggering and tremendous in its eschatological grandeur and judgement, but in point of fact when God did break through, when the Eternal, as it were, plunged into history, and eschatology was realized, it was a manifestation of Divine Love rather than of Divine Power—an illustration that the weakness of God is stronger than man. The glory of God flooded the earth when the Angels sang:

> *Peace on earth, and mercy mild,*
> *God and sinners reconciled.*

It was Love that came down at Christmas. The noblest possible expression of eschatology was this manifestation of the greatest fact about God—God is Love. People who were expecting in the first century a day of wrath and judgement (however and whenever such a day may come in the future) experienced a day of infinite mercy. God sent not His Son into the world to condemn the world, but that the world through Him might be saved. To quote a modern writer:

*He did not come to judge the world, He did not come to blame,*
*He did not only come to seek, it was to save He came.*
*And when we call Him Saviour, then we call Him by His Name.*

How are we best to define the Kingdom of God on earth? Though it is true that the Kingdom of Christ is not exactly a biblical term, there are a number of passages of scripture that would justify us in calling this new epoch, the Kingdom of Christ, as for instance when it is called the Kingdom of His dear Son.[6] In a sense Our Lord acted, as the Vicegerent of God, as St Paul puts it in the First Epistle to the Corinthians. There is a limitation to the reign of Christ. 'Then cometh the end, when he shall have delivered up the kingdom to God, even the Father; when he shall have put down all rule and all authority and power. For he must reign, till he hath put all enemies under his feet. . . . But when he saith all things are put under him, it is manifest that he is excepted, which did put all things under him. And when all things shall be subdued unto him, then shall the Son also himself be subject unto him that put all things under him, that God may be all in all.'[7] This passage implies that Jesus came into the world to overcome the Powers of Evil which defied the reign of God. His Mission was to conquer them, and on the cross[8] He did conquer, as St Paul says, principalities and powers and triumphed over them. Representing, as it were, his heavenly Father, He set up and extended His Kingdom in the world, a Kingdom which, having won, He will finally give back to the Father that God may be all in all. Hence we may well call the Kingdom of God on earth which created a new epoch in the world, through the Ministry of our Saviour, the Kingdom of Christ.[9]

[6] Colossians $1^{14}$.  [7] 1 Corinthians $15^{24-8}$.  [8] Colossians 2.

[9] This term will be generally used in these pages to describe the Kingdom of God on Earth.

**(See also 'Additional Note'**, p. 143, *infra.*)

## THE GOOD NEWS

Though the irruption of the Eschatological order into time and space is rightly described by Bultmann and others as a pure Act of God without human intervention or help, it actually worked through the Man Christ Jesus, who had taken humanity upon Him in order to fulfil the works of God: human beings surely were used and commissioned by Christ to preach His Kingdom, and to be the instruments in its expansion. They were to be the Light of the world and the Salt of the earth, and were commissioned to preach the Gospel to every creature. Their work in building up the kingdom, was of course God's work through them.

St Paul does not doubt that new conquests are to be won by Christ. How, we ask, when and where are they to be made? Evidently the Apostle foresaw future victories. The victory over principalities and powers on the Cross was not the last victory to be won by Jesus. When the final victory is gained, Christ will give the Kingdom He has won on Earth to the Father. In his letter to the Romans St Paul writes to Christian men, 'it is high time to awake out of sleep' and to 'put on the armour of light'. These too are the soldiers through whom the ever-present Captain of Salvation fights and conquers.

The Kingdom of God has arrived, said Jesus, but did it come to stay—what was the future of it? In the Lord's Prayer we say 'Thy kingdom come', hence the Kingdom of Christ is described at first sight paradoxically as both present and future, but if in fact the Kingdom was to have an earthly development it would seem that though it was present it would naturally also be future. There can be no doubt, however, that a future consummation of the Kingdom conceived in apocalyptic language was expected by early Christians. It is perhaps not wrong to emphasize the distinction just made between the Kingdom of God in its wider sense and the Kingdom of Christ on earth. The general opinion today that the early Church was looking for the immediate coming again of Christ in glory seems to have been somewhat exaggerated by the eschatological school of scholars.

Other facts are much more emphasized in the early preaching of Peter and Paul as recorded in the Acts of the Apostles. But whatever was the view of the Second Advent in the New Testament writings—a declining view—in actual practice the early Church organized for a continuance and development of the Kingdom of Christ on earth.

Some modern scholars argue that the parables of Jesus spoken by the seaside must be treated eschatologically and the end—the harvest—is the one thing to consider. But if they are taken together the common emphasis seems to be on the vitality, the unconquerable vitality of the word of the Kingdom. It matters not that some soil in which it is sown is hard and other weedy.

The slumber of the farmer who sowed the seed does not hamper its growth; even if the devil sows tares in the wheat the wheat will still develop. The smallness of the mustard seed does not hinder the size of tree which springs from it; only a little leaven is needed to quicken the whole lump.

Surely these parables teach that the Kingdom of God will develop and prevail whatever hindrances it meets. So our Lord taught His disciples. Then why? He commissioned them to preach; He visualized the spread of the Gospel over the world in such a way that He could speak of His feet-washing by Mary and of her precious gift as a fact which was to have a world-wide publicity. After His resurrection the disciples were sufficiently organized to fill a vacancy in their ranks. The Acts of the Apostles is the story of the development of the Jewish Church and the Gentile mission. There seems to be no compulsive sense of the sudden ending coming to the Church. On the other hand the Christians are co-workers with God for the establishment of His Kingdom. It is more easy to interpret the words of the Lord's Prayer—Thy kingdom come. Thy will be done in earth as it is in heaven—as a prayer for the extension of the Kingdom of Christ on earth, rather than as a prayer for the coming consummation of the Kingdom of God.

The Kingdom of Christ on earth and its future is well pictured in familiar hymns:

> *Hail to the Lord's Anointed;*
> *Great David's greater Son!*
> *Hail, in the time appointed,*
> *His reign on earth begun!*
> *He comes to break oppression,*
> *To set the captive free,*
> *To take away transgression,*
> *And rule in equity.*
>
> *He shall come down like showers*
> *Upon the fruitful earth:*
> *Love, joy, and hope, like flowers,*
> *Spring in His path to birth:*
> *Before Him, on the mountains,*
> *Shall peace the herald go;*
> *And righteousness in fountains,*
> *From hill to valley flow.*

And the future of that Kingdom is truly described in the confident words:

> *Jesus shall reign where'er the sun*
> *Doth his successive journeys run.*

Reconciliation, forgiveness of sins, is achieved through the love of God manifest and active in the death of Christ; Salvation is through His life. Our hope for final salvation is based on the fact of His risen life. 'I know that my Redeemer lives.'

Not only is our individual salvation secured by union with the living Christ, but social salvation also. When we live 'in Christ' we come to the Father in and through Him, and consequently into the Father's family which is the Kingdom of God on earth. It is the Kingdom of His dear Son into which we are translated when delivered from the powers of darkness.[10]

Though a mystical relation of the redeemed man to the living Saviour is a precious experience of the redeemed, the words 'in

---

[10] Colossians 1[13].

Christ' seem always to mean, as Dr C. H. Dodd asserts, 'in His body'. There is no *exclusive* mystical relation between the individual Christian with Christ as an individual. There is no mystical mingling of personalities. To be in Christ is to be a member of the Body of Christ. Our communion is not only with Him, but with His Community. No one in early Christianity claimed to be a Christian who was not a member of the Body of Christ—of His Community—of His Church.

The implications of this Social Fellowship are worked out in succeeding chapters: here it is sufficient to say that underlying St Paul's phrase, 'in Christ', is the teaching of our Lord that His Kingdom is the Father's family. The true conception of the Christian Gospel involves not only forgiveness through the death of Christ, but practical living in union with Christ in the social community He has created—as fellow workers with Him, fellow soldiers in His army, men pledged to seek first the Kingdom of God and His righteousness. Jesus not only died and rose again to be the Saviour of every man who trusts in Him but also to make a new world to be peopled by new people. Entrance into His Kingdom, He said, was open only to children, to newborn little ones who were greater than the greatest man in the old epoch. 'Old things have passed away. Yea, all things have become new.'

Our Lord's announcement that the Kingdom of God had come was the revolutionary declaration of a new world. His death and resurrection created new people with changed minds and a new outlook. New people were needed for that New World.

CHAPTER SIX

## THE TWOFOLD GOSPEL

*Rejoice, the Lord is King!*
  *Your Lord and King adore;*
*Mortals, give thanks, and sing,*
  *And triumph evermore:*

Lift up your heart, lift up your voice;
Rejoice; again I say, Rejoice.

*Jesus the Saviour reigns,*
  *The God of truth and love;*
*When He had purged our stains,*
  *He took His seat above:*

Lift up your heart, lift up your voice;
Rejoice; again I say, Rejoice.

*His kingdom cannot fail,*
  *He rules o'er earth and heaven;*
*The keys of death and hell*
  *Are to our Jesus given:*

Lift up your heart, lift up your voice;
Rejoice; again I say, Rejoice.

THE MUCH-QUOTED saying that there are two Gospels in t New Testament, the Gospel *of* Jesus and the Gospel *ab* Jesus, really expresses two aspects of one Gospel. It is true tl the Gospel of Jesus is the Good News of the Kingdom of G and of His heavenly Father which He preached; and that t Apostolic Gospel, especially that of St Paul, was about Je Himself and the Salvation that is to be found in Him. But is a mistake to think that Paul did not preach the Kingdom God or that Jesus was not the conscious Saviour of Man.

Jesus talked relatively little, though sufficiently about ] death and resurrection, but He did more than speak; He d and He rose again, and these facts of themselves spoke. Jesus was the giver of Salvation, and St Paul and the other Apostles were its recipients. Hence the Gospel which St Paul preaches is the witness he gives to the Good News as he puts it in a passage of Scripture: 'This is a faithful saying, and worthy of all acceptation, that Christ Jesus came into the world to save sinners.'

When Jesus commanded the Apostles to go into all the world and preach the Gospel, to every creature, the Good News that they were to declare was the Good News of the Kingdom of God. But also He said to them, 'Lo, I am with you alway, even unto the end of the world', and that to them was Good News, in some sense the best of all to them. The Gospel therefore that was preached is twofold in the sense that it is the Good News of the Kingdom of God on earth, and also the Good News that the King is risen and dwells amongst his people; but it is essentially the one Gospel of the person of Jesus and His message of the Kingdom.

The notion that the 'gospel about Jesus' was an apostolic innovation will not bear careful examination. When St Paul wrote 'Christ is all and in all' he was really giving the testimony of his own experience to the claims of Jesus. Jesus said 'Come unto ME... Follow ME... Believe in ME... *I* am the Way... *I* am the bread of life ... *I* am the water of life ... *I* am the good shepherd who gave his life for the sheep ... *I* am the light of the world'—that is to say: 'I am all and in all.'

'The Kingdom of God's dear Son'[1] into which Christians are 'translated' has come into this world and is here, now, but it so had a future on earth because Jesus, 'risen and living'[2] is with us alway.

Jesus is much more than an eminent teacher of important truths: He is Himself the Truth He teaches.[3] He is the WORD—the λόγος, who became flesh and is full of grace and truth. Always present Himself, He carries on His work and extends His Kingdom along with, and by means of, His followers.[4]

[1] Colossians 1:13.   [2] Matthew 28:20.   [3] John 1:14.
[4] See Chapters 8 and 9, *infra*.

His Kingdom would neither have meaning nor future if the King were not here. It is because He lives and must reign on earth[5] that we can pray, confident that our prayer will be answered,[6] to His Father and ours: 'Thy Kingdom come on earth.' So we ascribe glory to Him[7] 'Who loves us and who hath loosed us from our sins by the shedding of His blood—He hath made us a Kingdom[8] of priests for his God and Father'.

When we think of the rich evangelical message of St Paul and the early preachers of Christianity, one thing must never be forgotten, namely that many people in that day were expecting the coming of God to judge them, and thought about Him as the Judge of all the earth. The surprising thing is that when He did come in Christ, He did not come to judge them. He came in mercy—though St Paul and indeed all the writers and preachers of the New Testament continued to believe, as indeed we all must, that some time there must be a day of Judgement. The fact of history to be noted is that the form in which God came in the first century, was not that of a judge, but of a Father who was realized through His Beloved Son.

There are of course explicit references in Paul's writings, and in the Acts of the Apostles, as we have already seen in these pages, to the Kingdom of God. But underlying all his preaching, that Kingdom is assumed.

There are people who tell us that St Paul's relationship to the Fatherhood of God is very different from that of Jesus. Paul's writings lack the familiar notes with which Jesus always addresses God as His Father. But it is quite a mistake to think that Paul, because he uses the expression, did not preach the Fatherhood of God less commonly than Jesus did. Paul in his contacts with God discovered that he was dealing at that time not with a terrible judge administering a Law which was impossible for human beings to obey, but with a loving Father.

He expresses his sense of God's Fatherhood in his statements that God sent Jesus into the world to be the 'First-born of many

[5] Revelation 11$^{15}$.   [6] Matthew 6$^9$.
[7] Revelation 1$^{5-6}$ (Moffatt).   [8] Moffatt translates '*Realm*'.

brethren'. That God's Fatherhood is the common experience of His children is clearly taught in Romans 8, when men and women who have freshly realized that God pardons them their sins, almost at the beginning of their religious life, cry out to God: 'Abba! Father!' While the Apostle used the term Fatherhood less than his Master did, his continual preaching of the grace of God and His free gift to men, shows that he is thinking rather of 'Our Father' than of a judge.

Underlying the evangelical message of St Paul is always his realization of God's Fatherhood. His preaching indeed would be unintelligible unless we realized that salvation was the free gift of a Father and not a reward or wages for good conduct.

Perhaps the Gospel of St Paul—'My Gospel', as he calls it—is most effectively summarized in Romans 5[10]: 'If, when we were enemies, we were reconciled to God by the death of his Son, much more, being reconciled, we shall be saved by his life.' Both the reconciliation of men to God by the Death of Christ and the salvation of pardoned men by His risen life are ultimately in the preaching of Paul, an expression of God's free grace, that is to say, of His Fatherhood.

In the fifth chapter of the Epistle to the Romans, St Paul relates the saving works of Christ to the Love of God. In another epistle he tells us that God in Christ was reconciling the world to Himself. In His earthly life our Lord was always seeking and saving the lost and preaching His message of love, and through such words and deeds, His Father was reconciling the world to Himself. But the supreme act of reconciliation by which 'God commended His own love toward us was that while we were yet sinners, Christ died for us. It is the love of the Father which is manifested through the death of His Son, but it is not only a manifestation of the love of God in the death of Christ, but Love itself in action: 'The power of God unto salvation.'

Nothing is more amazing than the free pardon which God offers to all penitent men who will accept it. The danger of which Paul himself was not unconscious that men should as it were exploit the love of God and do evil, is one that always exists where this doctrine is taught. The Jews themselves said that a judge 'justifies the wicked in an abomination unto the Lord',[9] and yet Paul was continually saying that God, whom the Jews thought of as the Judge, justified the ungodly.

How can we wonder at the indignation of the Jews! After all, if God is a judge and only a judge, it would be His duty to administer the laws and to pass sentences upon those who disobeyed Him. But this according to Paul was just what, in this new epoch, God did not do. He did not act as a judge, but He acted as a Father. God was not reconciled to men because they were good, nor did He punish men because they were bad. He was not judge, but father, and loved them because they were His children. His gifts of love to the children of men were unconditional and unconditioned, though the capacity of people to accept them depended upon their penitence and faith; His gifts, as Jesus said, were like the shining of the sun and the falling of the rain upon just and unjust alike. This amazing grace of the heavenly Father, in the new epoch which came with Jesus Christ and His Kingdom, is contrasted by St Paul with times of which he so strangely says: 'God winked at.' When God's offer of free pardon to all men, whatever their condition, nation, or morality, through the death of His Son, is accepted, they become reconciled to God; or, in simpler language, are pardoned by Him.

The mistake has often been made in evangelical circles of identifying the forgiveness of sins with Salvation. The truth is, as this passage tells us, that the forgiven man is only starting on the road of Salvation. It is through his union with the Living Risen Christ that his salvation will be accomplished: 'How much more are we saved by His life.'

To understand how the Fatherhood of God stands behind these words, we need to think of God's relation to men as it is expressed in this chapter. In the third chapter of Romans

[9] Proverbs 17[18].

we are told that 'All have sinned and come short of the Glory of God'. That is the universal fate, as we see again in the fifth chapter, of the children of Adam. But what is this glory of which we have all fallen short? Must we think of it as celestial glory. I think not. In 1 Corinthians 9 St Paul says that man himself is 'the glory and image of God'. Man, that is to say as God made him, made in His image. That, Paul says, is the glory of God. To fall short therefore of the glory of God, is to fall short of the image of God in which we were created. That is the lot of all men. We have failed to be the men God meant us to be. There is one exception to this universal human failure; namely Jesus Himself. He has lived a human life perfectly. He is the man God meant Him to be.

God looks at human beings, and so far as they are failures He offers them free pardon, because He sees them as they may be when He sees Jesus. Dr C. H. Dodd gives us a hint here which he does not develop, and which is worth noting: 'A sense of worth in the Beloved is perhaps the characteristic of parental love which most justifies the use of the term Fatherhood.'

God believes in His children in spite of their failure because He knows one man has succeeded. God sees what we are—failures—and forgives us. But He also sees what we can be and what in Christ, we may be. The extreme Calvinistic view of man's total depravity is not really a Pauline doctrine. Deeper than a man's original sin, is his original righteousness. We have all defaced the image of God in which we were made and come short of His glory. But no man entirely effaces it.

> *What I could never be*
> *What men ignored in me*
> *That was I worth to Him whose wheel the pitcher shaped.*

Or to quote the great words of Goethe: '*Werde was du bist*' (Become what you are). Salvation is the educational work by which a forgiven man through union with Christ can reach up again to the glory that is the image of God from which he has fallen. As St Paul says, we are changed by beholding, from glory to glory, into the image of the Lord. And the image of the Lord is that glory of the only-begotten son of God, which, as St John says, men beheld 'full of grace and truth'.

In our country there have been, roughly speaking, two methods of education. The traditional one was that of the rod. Ancient schoolmasters tried hard to 'whip the offending Adam out of him'. A great change came in English public-school life when Dr Arnold at Rugby School thought a better way was to put a boy on his honour. I had the misfortune to be trained under both methods. I remember a master at my school who gave the boys of his class a problem in algebra and said that if any boy failed to solve it, he would thrash him severely. He came to look at our answers and the first boy, my neighbour, whose paper he saw, was said to have failed, and the master thrashed him unmercifully. He then came on to me and found my answer was wrong, but the same as the boy he had thrashed, so he accused me of copying. But before he administered the punishment to me, he looked at the answer of the next boy, and he found that, too, was the same. It then occurred to him that there must be something strange in this identity of solutions and he worked out the problem again, and found that we were right and he was wrong. I record this story because of what he said to the boy whom he had brutally mauled: 'I shall make no apology, you can take that thrashing on account, you are sure to deserve it tomorrow.'

A theory which regards evil as the necessary course for a boy to pursue is utterly false. We had another master who told us that he treated us as gentlemen and put us on our honour. I confess that I often thought that he did not know us very well. But his method was the right method. It is the method of grace rather than of the rod that Paul, to his great surprise, found in his heavenly Father.

Readers of Ibsen's great drama, *Peer Gynt*, will remember how that Norwegian scoundrel had, notwithstanding the evil things that he did, a sort of dream life which cherished goodness. But he decided not to be himself the man of his own ideals, but to be to himself enough. That is to say, to live a life of worldly greed. The drama shows how he tried to make compromises between the two selves, but failed to be the man God made him to be. After a life of great, though, dishonourable success, he goes back to his native Norway, and is wrecked in a storm on the Norwegian coast. The ruined desperate man meets a mythological character called the Buttonmoulder, who says his work is to merge buttons into the mass which have lost their loops. And he has a ladle for the purpose. He accuses Peer Gynt of being such a loopless button. A man who had lost his identity, and unless he could find someone to witness to it, must go into the ladle. Peer Gynt in desperation tries to find someone who can prove his identity, but fails. Once or twice the Buttonmoulder has given him another chance, but now the next time they meet, unless he can prove his identity there is nothing for him but the ladle. Then he sees sitting outside the cottage on the hillside, an old woman, who is Solveig, who had been the girl whom he had loved and forsaken years before. And in desperation he cries to her:

P. Can you answer riddles?
S. Tell me them.
P. Tell them to be sure. Can'st thou tell me where Peer Gynt has been since we parted?
S. Been?
P. With his destiny seal on his brow.
Been as in God's sight he first sprang forth.
Can'st thou tell me?—If not . . .
S. Oh that riddle is easy.
P. Tell me what thou knowest.
Where was I the whole man the true man.
S. In my faith, in my hope, in my love.

Is not this a parable of God's Love of Humanity. The real men and women are not the failures who have come short of the glory of God, but the men and women whom He created in His own image and purposed to be like His Son.

May we not ask, speaking after the manner of men, whether the Heavenly Father's hope for His children has any better grounds of fulfilment than those of any other affectionate parent? The answer is that God, when He has freely pardoned our sins and shortcomings, sees us not in Adam, guilty and sinful, but in Christ, the representative of man as God created man to be. He sees us united to Christ who is 'the firstborn of many brethren', to whose image the whole family is to conform.[10]

'In Christ' (ἐν Χριστῷ) is the Apostle's favourite and most often repeated phrase. He not only sees 'in Christ' man as He made man to be, but 'in Christ'—in our union with Christ—God sees men as they may be and can be. When pardoned men begin to walk not after the flesh but after the Spirit,[11] that is when they are possessed by the Spirit of His Son, then the heavenly Father—I write again after the manner of men—has a guarantee for His hope of their salvation. It is thus that men who are 'in Christ'—united with Him—are changed from glory to glory into His image.[12] Those who are identified with Christ—united with Him—He raises by the power of His resurrection into heavenly places 'in Christ Jesus'.[13]

The Father's hope for our salvation assumes, and is grounded upon, the resurrection of Jesus from the dead. But it is not only on the resurrection itself that our salvation depends, but on the fact that the risen Saviour lives amongst His people always to guide and guard them, that they may grow continually in the grace and knowledge of their Lord and Saviour.[14] Because He lives we can, when united with Him, live the life of the Spirit. Christ is 'all in all' to His people. They may well sing:

> *Thou of life the fountain art,*
> *Freely let me take of Thee.*

[10] Romans 8.   [11] ibid., verses 1-6.   [12] 2 Corinthians.
[13] Ephesians 1 and 2.   [14] 2 Peter.

CHAPTER SEVEN

# THE CHRISTIAN REVOLUTION

*'Twixt the mount and multitude
Doing or receiving good.*

---

*Arm yourselves with all the mind
That was in Christ, your Head.*

THE ANNOUNCEMENT of Jesus that the Kingdom of God had come, involved such a trans-valuation of values that it may be well called the most revolutionary sentence ever spoken. Jesus did not outline a form of government, but announced principles of the most revolutionary character. After two thousand years we cannot perhaps feel the force of them so vividly as the people to whom they were first announced. Furthermore, application or partial application of some of these principles in national governments makes a difference in our apprehension of them, although the thorough practice of them today would turn upside down any government on earth. These principles, especially enunciated in the Sermon on the Mount, are left for us to implement. The modern eschatological school, it is true, has a different conception of the Kingdom of God. The sermon on the Mount is a sufficient and effective answer to eschatological extravagances.

Mr Gwylym Griffith in his illuminating book on John Bunyan[1] has brought to light a pamphlet of Bunyan's, *The Holy City*, written during one of his imprisonments. It gives an unexpected picture of the largeness of Bunyan's mind and outlook. Here we see a man no mere dreamer far removed from the illiterate tinker whom some regard him to be; a man who analyses deeply the weaknesses of the Church of his own days and sets forth a noble conception of what it might become and do.

[1] pp. 163ff.

Bunyan employed vigorously the puritan invective against the hated and dreaded Church of Rome and did not fail to speak the language which in the phrase of Mr Griffith has been localized under the name Billingsgate. Notwithstanding his language, however, he was evidently impressed with the dignity and majesty of the medieval Church. Although a faithful son of the Reformation, 'it belonged to his untutored wisdom' to recognize that to break up the papal unity and call the fragments Protestantism was no solution of the world's problem. He saw no advantage in a deliverance from religious coercion which resulted in an era of religious confusion.

The warring sects and the secondary and even trifling reasons for which they broke communion with each other infuriated Bunyan. Baptism by immersion, though Bunyan was a Baptist himself, he regarded as an inadequate cause of separation. So much did he protest against the rigidity of the leading Anabaptists of his day that he was ostracized by them. In these matters he was far ahead of his times. His enthusiasm for Christian union among Protestants was at least three hundred years before his time. Indeed we shall be lucky if even after a like period the disgraceful divisions of Christianity are healed.

Bunyan, who regarded the Reformation as the commencement of a new Christian era, wrote his pamphlet under three heads: (1) Altar Work; (2) Temple Work; (3) City Work. He regarded the Reformation doctrines of personal salvation as the consummation of Altar work. He is chiefly concerned with what he calls Temple work by which he means the unification of the violently quarrelsome sects of his day. Temple work implies a new construction of Christian unity, the realization of one Church. So broad was his outlook that he would have welcomed any truly Christian Roman Catholic into the fellowship. 'My heart and the door of our congregation are open to receive them into closest fellowship with us.' Again, he says, 'It is darkness that keepeth God's people from knowing one another and makes them stand at so great a distance both in judgement and affections', but when the light shines, 'it shall not be then, as now, a Papish doctrine, a Quaker's doctrine, a prelatical doctrine and the Presbyter, Independent, and Anabaptist, thus distinguished and thus confounded and destroying', but undivided fellowship ruled by love.

City work was the final hope of Bunyan. The Holy City he thought would come into being after the united Church had exemplified by its life the will of God, and had become a pattern for the world as it should be. Then the City of God and the Kingship of Christ would be acknowledged by the whole world. But until the ideal was materialized, Bunyan thought the kings of the earth probably would not submit to it, but when the city was once established he believed that its sheer beauty would convince all men and that literally the Kingdoms of this world would become the Kingdom of one God and His Christ. This is not an allegory written under the similitude of a dream, but the vital hope of Bunyan when he was fully awake. May we not still be inspired by Bunyan's hope and be sure that when the principles of the Sermon on the Mount are implemented by the followers of Christ, the City of God will be established on the earth.

I propose to use the headings of Bunyan's pamphlet, without using his arguments, as a classification of the revolutionary principles of the Sermon on the Mount.

(a) *The Altar Work.* The first thing to be noticed is our Lord's emphasis on personal religion which is and must remain fundamental through all Christian service. There are two things to be said about this. The first claim of Jesus is that he conserves what is good in the ancient law and fulfils the true meaning of the law even when He seems to break it.

He is not careful about the shell which has of course preserved the life. But it is only by breaking the shell that the bird can issue forth. The real meaning and purpose of the egg is the bird, and our Lord breaks ancient shells in order to liberate life.

But most of all we notice His stress on the interior life. He denounces the futility of mere outward forms and shows how deep-seated evil is in the heart of men, where it must be met and conquered. So it is that He finds murder, adultery, revenge in anger, unchaste thoughts and hatred. Only by the cleansing of the interior life can a man truly do that which is well-pleasing in the sight of God. A radical change of heart and mind are essential facts in the new order established by Jesus, and the positive character of dealing with these inner evils is stressed by His emphasis on love, even of the people who are around us. Love is to take the place of every sort of revenge and hatred of our enemies. The perfection to which He calls men is a perfection in love as can be seen by the parallel of St Luke's gospel where, instead of Matthew's words 'Be ye perfect as your Father in heaven is perfect', we read: 'Be ye therefore merciful as your Father in heaven is merciful.' The principles of sheer sincerity, of absolute truth, have never been demanded so drastically of religious men. Christ's requirements of plain 'nay, nay' and 'yea, yea' emphasizes his expectation that the truthfulness of a Christian should be self-evident.

(*b*) *The Temple Work.* The unification of the people of God was to John Bunyan a step toward the City of God. In other words, Christianity can never be regarded as a purely individualistic relation to God. The most important words in the Sermon on the Mount are probably those of the Lord's Prayer. The sociality of Christianity is demonstrated by both of its first two words, 'Our' and 'Father'. There is nothing more necessary to understand in our Lord's teaching than the central emphasis which is put on the word 'Father'. It is probably true that the humanistic school of the nineteenth century did sentimentalize this word, but the reaction in the dominant eschatologist of our time seriously underestimates our Lord's conception of the fatherhood of God. Is it realized that He never spoke to God except to call him 'Father', with the one exception of His words on the Cross, which were a quotation from another man's writing, when He said, 'My God, my God, why hast thou forsaken me'? In the Sermon on the Mount alone Jesus uses the word 'Father' eleven times. While it is not true to say, as some have said, that the word 'Father' in relation to God was first used by Jesus, it is true to say that he gave to the word a new significance. The nineteenth-century sentimentality of some uses of the word 'Father', modelled on a modern conception of indulgence in fatherhood, was foreign to the days of Jesus. Reverence of the father of a human family, and his kingship in it, was much more recognized than in nineteenth-century England or America. The completely tender way in which Jesus thinks of His Father in heaven and treats Him in the way anyone else treats a father, is an outstanding feature in the life of Jesus, and His desire to share the fatherhood of God with which He uses such phrases as, 'For your heavenly father knoweth that ye have need of these things'[2] or 'Behold the fowls of the air, they sow not nor reap, yet your heavenly father feedeth them. Are ye not much better than they?'[3] or 'If ye then, being evil, know how to give good gifts to your children, how much more shall your heavenly father give good gifts to them that ask Him?'[4]

Nor must it be forgotten that Jesus, when He claimed that no man knoweth the Father except the Son and to whomsoever the Son willeth to reveal Him, at the same time invited all labouring and troubled people to come to Him for rest.[5] Could there be anything but peace of mind for people who really believe that the God of all power was their father in heaven? The pardoning love of God is love of His children, not because they are good, but because they are His children, so that he sends sunshine and rain on the good and evil alike. This is a startling and unique revelation of God's fatherly mercy without which it is impossible to understand the teaching of Jesus.

The Fatherhood of God involves a family of God. If you come to your heavenly Father you cannot evade the responsibilities of His family. Mysticism is a word of very various uses but in its most distinctive form it stands for a relation of the soul to God as of an individual to an individual. This is really an impossible relationship because God is Himself a plurality and a Holy Trinity, and all men only realize personality through their relation to other men. There was, of course, a tendency

[2] Matthew $6^{32}$.  [3] ibid., verse 26.  [4] ibid., $7^{11}$.  [5] ibid., $11^{25-30}$.

THE CHRISTIAN REVOLUTION 77

in some of the Reformation teaching so to stress the relation of the soul to God as to ignore the fact that wherever the soul comes into contact with God it comes into contact with the heavenly Father, and therefore family obligations cannot be evaded. This is the very essence of the meaning of the Church, as we shall see in the next chapter, but what is necessary to understand is that to believe in a heavenly Father is to believe in the brotherhood of all those who acknowledge that fatherhood, and hence any denominational differences—the savagery of which shocked John Bunyan nearly three hundred years ago—are entirely inconsistent with any valid relation to the heavenly Father and to His family. While this sense of the family of God has a special application to the Church, it has much wider applications to the Kingdom of Christ on earth, for the extension of which Christian men must fight. It is impossible to further the interests of the Kingdom of God with any adequate words unless those who profess to be His children show true union and fellowship, and what so interested John Bunyan was the necessity, in spite of the savage sectarianism of his time, to achieve some constructive spiritual union which would enable the followers of Jesus, through His leadership, to make the kingdoms of this world the kingdoms of our God and of His Christ.

It is important as we say the Lord's Prayer, to catch the significance of the words, 'Thy Kingdom come', to ask ourselves what is the Kingdom of the heavenly Father, for in the prayer we say, 'Our Father', 'Thy Kingdom come'. It is a Father's kingdom we are thinking of and praying for, and a Father's Kingdom is the family—where He rules and rules by love.

In this family sense the Church should be the model of the Kingdom of Christ on earth. The one rule which is stressed in the Sermon on the Mount is that of Love. This is characteristic of all early Christianity. The twelfth to fourteenth chapters of the first Epistle to the Corinthians, which deal with the differences which imperilled the early Church, clearly show that the one governing power that counts is love, and so, spatchcocked into the midst of discussions of Church policy, St Paul writes his inimitable hymn of the love which He calls 'the more excellent way'. I believe that much the most fitting description of the Kingdom of Christ is just simply 'the family of the heavenly Father'. Where our Lord uses or is said to have used apocalyptic language, which nobody can really understand, about the Kingdom of God, it would be a great gain if people used the words, 'Our Father, Thy kingdom come', remembering that a Father's kingdom is a family, for in these words is the true key of interpretation.

(c) *The City Work.* Now the Church of Christ, the model family of God on earth, becomes the instrument through which Our Saviour establishes His Kingdom on earth. It is only by the family of God that some of the highest ideals of human society can be achieved. The favourite saying of the French revolution—*Liberté! Egalité! et Fraternité!*—can never be realized except in the family of God. If the individual has liberty, equality is sacrificed. If equality is established, individual liberty must be suppressed. Fraternity suggests the family, but fraternity is a meaningless word apart from paternity. The Christian conception of the family, properly worked out, is the only conception that can preserve the rights of the individual along with the claims of the community.

The family conception of human society creates a new ethic different from that of the law courts—the ethic of love. Two of the parables of Jesus bring this out. In the parable of the Prodigal Son our sympathies naturally go to the poor fellow who comes home in such distress and is received again by a loving father, and we feel indignation with the man who clamours for his own rights and really denies his obligations to his brother and is quite alienated from his father's heart. But in the parable of the Labourers in the Vineyard it is difficult for us not to feel sympathy with the men who have borne the heat and burden of the day, when they say that it is not fair that a man who has done only one hour's work has the same payment as theirs. It is only in the family that the action of the master of the vineyard could be justified, and yet the complaint of the labourers is essentially that of the elder brother of the other parable, and the reason why we are unsympathetic with him is simply that family relationships are different from those of the labour yard. We are a long way even today from the family ethic which is evident in the revolutionary principles of the Sermon on the Mount.

It must never be forgotten that even the forgiveness of God is forfeited by men who do not forgive their brothers. No more dreadful words of Jesus are recorded than those by which He applies the parable of the unmerciful servant: 'So likewise shall my heavenly Father do also unto you, if ye from your hearts forgive not every one his brother their trespasses.'[6]

Dreams of the City of God are to be found in the Old Testament. That of the book of Zechariah is especially attractive. There we read of an ideal city which is without walls or fortifications except for Jehovah Himself, who is to be a protecting wall of fire; it is to be a city of peace for all nations, extended and expanded, indeed a sort of garden city. His dream is of a peaceful place in war-like days, where the old men are to be found with their staffs in their hands and the little children play in the streets. This is a beautiful figure of a peaceful city in times of slaughter, when men did not reach old age and when there were few children to play. And then in the chapter appended to Zechariah's writing is the figure of a peaceful king who comes, not riding on a war horse, but, in words made familiar by their gospel application to Jesus, sitting on an ass—which was a symbol of peace. The human agents in the city, Zerubbabel the prince and Joshua the priest, are to govern the city, but it is not by their skill or wisdom that the city is to be governed. 'Not by might, nor by power, but by my spirit', saith the Lord.

Or we think of the apocalyptic dream of the twenty-first chapter of the Book of Revelation, which describes in glowing imagery the millenial city of God come down to earth from heaven with its golden streets and pearly gates and the river of

[6] Matthew 18$^{23-35}$.

the water of life, with its miraculous fruit-bearing trees upon its banks.

In both of these two dream cities there is a striking common feature: 'Nought that defileth shall enter in', says the apocalyptist, and the presence of sin is to be expelled from Zechariah's city, where the woman who is sin is sealed up into a grotesque vessel and carried away from the city into Babylon, her native place, which the prophet satirically suggests is her real home.

This leads us to the most important fact that human ideals are ruined by the sinful will of men. The fact that prevents the dreams of the prophets coming true is the fact of sin, and no valid conception of the City of God is possible unless human sin is dealt with. I remember once in a discussion on the Brains Trust of the B.B.C. that someone asked a question about the hindrance that human sin caused to social regeneration, and Mr Bertrand Russell said somewhat snappishly: 'We shall not get much farther if we talk about sin.' May I suggest we shall not get on at all unless we do, for this is the great obstacle to all schemes of human betterment?

What is the chief hindrance to the establishment of the Kingdom of Christ—to the conquest of the Kingdom of Christ? Of course it is human sin. Our greatest historians see that today as they have never seen it before, as memorable passages of Arnold Toynbee show. The Regius Professor of Modern History at Cambridge, Professor Butterfield, quite definitely asserts that the study of history is the study of human sin. The tragical wars of the past, the great catastrophes which have ruined civilization after civilization, issue from pride, ambition, greed, lust and wickedness of rulers, not only of kings and emperors, but of republics and peoples as well. Even Gibbon points out that human history is the story of the crimes, follies and misfortunes of mankind. Sin is the great obstacle, and yet when we think about the future we think very little about the necessary eradication of the evil in human nature, which prevents the conquest, or at least hampers the campaigns of the Kingdom of God.

A recent work of Dr C. E. M. Joad on Bernard Shaw refers

to his own conversion to Christianity as a result of his repudiation of the shallow doctrine of Bernard Shaw. Shaw's teaching was that evil is the consequence of poverty and of bad environment. The elimination of such disadvantages—he believed and taught—would exterminate evil. Dr Joad, when he discovered that this was a false conception, came to the conclusion that the Christian doctrine of original sin was the true account of evil. 'Original Sin . . . is the fault and corruption of the nature of every man, that naturally is engendered of the offspring of Adam.'

I say little in this book about sin, and certainly do and will emphasize the positive rather than the negative sides of Christianity, not because I ignore sin, but because I believe that the best way of overcoming it is by the positive force of love. One of the most remarkable sayings of our time is that by Mr Bertrand Russell in a recent lecture, although he hesitated to say it: that what is most needed today is a revival of old-fashioned Christian Love. Some years ago in a book of his, *Scientific Outlook*, he said that he dreaded the future of the world that science would create unless knowledge were qualified by love. The one troublesome fact is that Mr Bertrand Russell has done as much as most men to belittle the springs of Christian Love. Christian Love will not exist and can never come into being if Christianity is undermined. And it must not be forgotten that the great fact of love is Redeeming Love. It is when a sinful man realizes the meaning of Redeeming Love that he says with Charles Wesley: 'Amazing love.' Hence, while we think of the dreams of good men, we cannot but realize their futility unless this problem is dealt with, and we must never forget, when we dwell upon the Gospel of Jesus, that primarily He was the Lamb of God which takes away the sin of the world. His conception of the Kingdom of His Father is based upon His redemptive power.

Is the Kingdom of the heavenly Father, the family of God which Jesus says has come into the world, anything more than a dream? When, for instance, in time of war, we read the sixth chapter of St Matthew's Gospel where we are exhorted to a trust in God that knows no anxiety and does not think of the morrow, in such tragical times as this through which our generation has passed, does it not seem that such a world is nothing but the dream of a poet? And yet here we are dealing with facts that can be realized if once men believe in the Kingdom of God as a Divine Family. If the time ever came when men do the will of God as the angels do it, poverty would necessarily be banished. The efforts made in our time to banish poverty have not been without a measure of success, largely owing to the Social conscience which Christianity has done more to create than any other force in the world. But the danger of a merely secular state which can give no lasting satisfaction to men, who sooner or later find an insatiable hunger for more than material things, is one that a true conception of the Kingdom of God, and that only, can defeat.

Our Lord compared a foolish and a wise man with houses, one built on the sands, and the other on the rock; but this comparison applies to the civilizations of the world. Every civilization in the world has perished so far, and perished because it has been founded on movable sands—worldly, political maxims, on military force, on political compromise, all of which are unstable foundations.

The one structure which has lasted for 2000 years is the Church of Christ, against which the gates of Hell will not prevail. The only sound structure of Human Society is the family. And the Society which is founded on Christ and kept alive by His Spirit is founded upon a rock and cannot be moved.

Let us then think of the City of God indicated in the principles of the Sermon on the Mount.

Let us consider the new aristocracy and we shall see how revolutionary the Kingdom is. It is described in the Beatitudes. In his literary study of the Bible, Dr R. G. Moulton regards the first Beatitude—'Blessed are the poor in spirit for theirs is the Kingdom of Heaven'—as *the* Beatitude, and the other seven as descriptions of it. St Luke's version is 'Blessed are the poor', but the Aramaic word for 'poor' is not only applied to the economic poor; St Matthew's expression seems to describe more truly the mind of Christ. The people who have the spirit of the poor are blessed, and their blessing lies in the fact that they are meek, that they hunger and thirst after righteousness, that they are merciful, that they have pure (simple) hearts. They have much to mourn over, and they mourn. They are the peacemakers, not mere talkers about peace, but those who construct peace. They are persecuted, reviled in the succession of all the prophets who have suffered in the past, and this makes them blessed. What a reversal! How the conception of the Beatitude of such people overturns all mundane conceptions of aristocracy! It is not the military man or the statesman, or the hereditary noble, or the plutocrat, or even the Rabbi, the man of learning whom Jesus characterizes as the Blessed in the Kingdom of God, but the people who have been abased and crushed, simple, humble, pure hearted, meek people, who shall inherit the earth. When properly understood, it is a most amazing thing that these people, socially at the very bottom of society, are to be the new aristocracy. And yet as we look back at the history of the Christian Church, how much they have counted. One of the significant sayings of Berdyaev is that the hierarchies do not carry the Church, but the Church carries the hierarchies. Cardinals, Bishops and officials of all sorts and kinds have often enough abused their trust, but the Church goes on because of its saints and martyrs, Berdyaev thinks. Above all in all centuries, however corrupt the Church in high places has been, there has been a continuous body of simple people who have lived apostolic lives and have made their quiet but powerful witness to Christ their Saviour. These people, in the eyes of God, are the true aristocracy of the Kingdom. The man who serves most is the man whom Christ chooses out of the greatest in the Kingdom of God, who is so humble, lowly, poor in spirit, that he is that very little child who enters into the Kingdom of Heaven.

These are the people—the sort of people to whom Jesus was

speaking—whom He calls the 'salt of the earth' and 'the light of the world'.

For this new and revolutionary kingdom our Lord requires new people, and it is a significant fact that he emphasizes this at the beginning of His Ministry. In Galilee he said that new bottles were required for new wine and that patch-work garments were of little use. In His earlier Ministry in Jerusalem, when Nicodemus (obviously interested in the teaching of Jesus of which He had heard or perhaps even heard himself) came for information by night to this new teacher, he was told that he could not have any conception of the kingdom of Christ unless he became a little child. There is not a more notable word of Jesus than His saying: 'Except ye be converted, and become as little children, ye shall not enter into the kingdom of heaven.' Entirely new people were needed for the new Kingdom. Ancient prejudices and conceptions were impossible hindrances to the realization of what is meant. Regeneration is usually spoken of as a personal requirement by Jesus—as Wesley calls it, 'a change in the disposition of the heart'—but we must not forget that the Kingdom of God, the irruption of the eternal order into the world of time and space, involves a regenerated world as well as regenerated individuals. New people are needed for a new world.

Nicodemus was confounded by our Lord's statement. He would have had no objection to becoming a little child, but he did not know how that could be accomplished. Jesus told him, and His message was nobly put, whether the words are those of the fourth evangelist as some think, or are those of Jesus Himself: 'God so loved the world, that he gave his only begotten Son, that whosoever believeth in him should not perish, but have everlasting life.' That is to say—trust in the unspeakable love of God which gives life. The New world is created by people who fall in love, by those who accept the wooing of the divine Lover, who listen to the voice of one who cries: 'How shall I let thee go, how shall I give thee up?' Human love gives to us the true picture of the divine love.

When Miranda, in love with Ferdinand, waking up saw a new world and said, 'O brave new world that has such goodly creatures in it', it was because of her love which made all things new, and so it is with the love of God in Christ. We can but, with Charles Wesley, wonder at it—'He hath loved, He hath loved us, we cannot tell why.' Such a love is always as Wesley said, 'amazing love'. It creates a new world—a magic world, the world of the little child. 'Know you what it is to be a child?' asks Francis Thompson: 'It is to be something very different from the man of today. It is to have a spirit yet streaming from the waters of baptism; it is to believe in love, to believe in loveliness, to believe in belief; it is to be so little that the elves can reach to whisper in your ear; it is to turn pumpkins into coaches, and mice into horses, lowness into loftiness, and nothing into everything, for each child has its fairy godmother in its own soul; it is to live in a nutshell and to count yourself the king of infinite space; it is

> *To see a World in a Grain of Sand,*
> *And Heaven in a Wild Flower,*
> *Hold Infinity in the palm of your hand,*
> *And Eternity in an hour.*

New people are required for the revolutionary Kingdom of Jesus.

This magical world is the world of the greatest of all revolutions. God's love—a fatherhood—is its central fact. The human race is ultimately to realize that it is the family of God. Love is to take the place of hate and vengeance, but if such a world is ever to be realized, the responsibilities of the followers are overwhelming. Many times in the past they have died for their faith, and the same witness to it can win new victories, but if the Kingdom of God is ever to prevail over the kingdoms of this world the people who are His conscious subjects must be united together in holy love. Their divisions to this day are the greatest hindrance to the realization of His Kingdom. The commission to preach the Gospel to every creature and the promise of the presence of the risen Saviour are the guarantees of ultimate victory. The process seems very slow and often very disappointing, but we must not forget that a thousand years is but as a day to Him who is our Leader and who has said: 'Fear not, little flock; for it is your Father's good pleasure to give you the kingdom.'

CHAPTER EIGHT

## THE FAMILY OF GOD

*Let all the Saints terrestrial sing,*
   *With those to glory gone;*
*For all the servants to our King,*
   *In earth and heaven, are one.*

*One family we dwell in Him,*
   *One Church, above, beneath,*
*Though now divided by the stream,*
   *The narrow stream of death:*
*One army of the living God,*
   *To His command we bow;*
*Part of His host have crossed the flood,*
   *And part are crossing now.*

---

*Love, like death, hath all destroyed,*
*Rendered all distinctions void;*
*Names, and sects, and parties fall:*
*Thou, O Christ, art all in all.*

IT WAS once the custom of old-fashioned evangelists, and indeed of many other people, to make a distinction between Jesus Christ and His Church. 'Come to Jesus', they used to say, and do not worry about the Church. The antithesis, Christianity or Churchianity, is not so frequently heard today, and in any case it is a very shallow one which will not bear analysis. An over-emphasis was put on the Gospel in reaction from over-emphasis in some quarters on the Church. The truth is, of course, that any man who comes to Jesus, the Elder Brother of the family of God, thereby comes to the Church. In the first Christian century, Church and Christianity were practically identical terms. No one would have been considered a Christian, or would have thought of himself as being one, who was not baptized and received into the Christian Community.

Much depends no doubt upon the definition of the term 'Church', but of the Church as it will be described in these pages, it would certainly be true to say there is no salvation outside it. When a man really comes through Christ to His Father he comes, not to an isolated and distant Deity, but to the Father of a family, to a social God. It is really impossible for a man to accept Christ and to be accepted by Him without entering into His Family—the Christian Brotherhood. We are not exclusive individuals dealing with an exclusive and solitary God. We are human beings, members of a human society, in contact with God—Father, Son, and Holy Ghost—and with His family. To accept God is to accept His Family, and we think of God the Father of our Lord and Saviour Jesus Christ, and to accept Him as our Father is to accept Brotherhood in His Family, and His Church is His family.

The conception of religion, for instance, of Professor A. N. Whitehead, that it is purely a private matter, is not the Christian conception. While there is much that is lofty and noble in mysticism, the term 'mystic' can only be applied in a qualified sense to Christians. The 'Mystic Way' is a way of renunciation and discipline whereby the individual gradually overcomes the flesh, and ultimately so liberates the spirit by his efforts that he may come into contact with the One God. Mr Aldous Huxley, who has given us a contracted but noble expression of mysticism in his book *Grey Eminence,* has richly illustrated with illuminating comments the mysticism he teaches. In his *Perennial Philosophy* he seems to dislike what is called Christian Mysticism, because he feels that the true mystic transcends the personal and human side of Christianity which he thinks sentimentalizes mysticism. A value of these statements of Aldous Huxley is that he shows clearly enough the difference between mysticism and evangelical Christianity. He chooses mysticism as the nobler way. To the Christian, God is a father; salvation is through His grace and not through human effort. However much Huxley may emphasize his view that the highest can only be reached by human beings, through effort and discipline, we affirm that the Christian revelation is of a God of Love, and while discipline, even to following of Christ by taking up His Cross, must always be emphasized, Jesus did say: 'Take my yoke upon you ... for my yoke is easy, and my burden is light.'

The Mystic Way, by which an individual travels to his lonely God, would obviously make the Church superfluous. To the pure mystic the statement that there is no salvation outside the Church, must seem meaningless and perhaps pernicious. Moreover, this saying has often been resented by Protestants who put their emphasis on 'the simple Gospel' which, apart from the Church, they regard as sufficient for all their needs. And the Protestant objection has much justification when the Church as defined by Roman Catholics is *the* Church, outside of which there is no salvation. The Protestant criticism arises much more from differences with the Church of Rome than from a failure to realize the social and fraternal obligations of Christians to their fellow Christians.

While we reject the solitary individualism of the mystic way on account of the necessary sociality of Christianity, we must not ignore the earnestness of the mystic's quest for God. There is a possibility which has too often been illustrated in modern Free Church services of so emphasizing the sociality of the Church, because of the family implications of the Fatherhood of God, as to forget that the Father of the Family is God, High and Lofty, to be adored and worshipped.

It is said of Gandhi that during his residence in South Africa he repudiated Methodist services because he regarded them rather as social entertainments than as the worship of God. If this be true, no more serious criticism of Methodism has ever been made. Though we hope that Gandhi suffered from a wrong impression of South African Methodism, we cannot deny that the conception of well meant, ''earty, 'omely and 'appy' services, risks a forgetfulness of the reverence which is essential. The primary importance of the worship of God is a fundamental tenet of the Holy Catholic Church, which has been preserved in the Roman and Greek communions by Eucharistic Devotions, and which was equally emphasized by the Fathers of the Reformation in their exaltation of the Bible as the living Word of God. In the modern Free Churches, however, there is an unquestionable tendency to a disintegrating subjectivity in worship. Professor Bisset Pratt, in his illuminating study of the Psychology of Religion—though himself a Protestant—contrasts Roman and Protestant services. The object of a Roman priest he says, is to worship God, and to see that such worship is devoutly conducted, with such ceremony and ritual as honours God. The idea of the Protestant minister, he thinks, is to instruct and edify man, and he rightly claims that the Protestant in this matter can learn from the Roman. While it is impossible for the Protestant to point to the Wafer, and say, 'God is here, adore Him', as the Catholic does, he can sing, with the Protestant Fathers:

> *Lo! God is here! let us adore,*
> *And own how dreadful is this place;*

or again:

> *Heaven comes down, our souls to greet,*
> *And glory crowns the Mercy Seat.*

The belief that God comes to his Temple to every place of worship, may be more easily evoked by the Roman's belief in His localization in the wafer, but we must never permit our disbelief in that localization to destroy our faith and awe in the presence of God. The wonder with which we claim His Fatherhood, and the joy, is surely deepened when we realize 'This awful God is ours'. The truth is that the time comes when we have no longer power to edify men if we ignore the fundamental fact of God. As has been shown in Chapter 1, nothing was more manifest in the Evangelical Revival of the eighteenth century than its fundamental theology and Eucharistic worship. There can be no future for any Christian organization which drowns reverence in mere sociability. God and the worship of God are fundamental facts in the life of the Church.

The Holy Catholic Church, which is much wider than the Roman Communion, can never do better, in any age or place, than to sing:

*We praise Thee, O God: we acknowledge Thee to be the Lord.*
*All the earth doth worship Thee: the Father Everlasting.*

What then is the Holy Catholic Church?

It is the Flock which the Great Shepherd of the sheep, when He was raised from the dead, gathered together. At the time of the Crucifixion, his followers were scattered like sheep without a shepherd—'A crowd of frightened sheep'. A shepherd was needed to make them into a flock, and that the Good Shepherd did. Sheep only become a flock when they are under the control of a shepherd. The Christian Church is entirely dependent upon the Life and Presence of the Good Shepherd. Not only must we rejoice in the Resurrection of Christ from the dead, but in the assurance which came to His disciples at Pentecost that He was living and present, to be with them even unto the end of the world. The early Church never thought of Jesus as dead, but always as one living in their midst. Indeed, at the very time when they were most conscious of His real and living presence, they called to memory the Lord's death and so proclaimed to the world the glorious scars of Him who lives for evermore.

The misunderstanding of the words of Jesus by St Jerome, whose mistaken translation in the Vulgate has been perpetuated in the English Authorized Version, has been a calamity to the Church. Jesus, as we now know, did not say that there should be One Shepherd and One Fold, but that He would collect together other sheep not of this fold that there might be One Shepherd and One Flock.

The exclusive claim of the Church of Rome would be stronger if Jesus had said that there should only be One Fold; but it is quite plain that He thinks of one flock but of many folds. When He says 'Sheep not of this fold', he is not thinking of stray sheep. In His time and country, flocks were taken by their shepherd to folds at night-time for security from wild beasts and robbers. The fold was generally an enclosure with some sort of earthen wall around it to which more than one flock could be taken by different shepherds, who in the morning led them out to pasture, each flock knowing the voice of its own shepherd, and following him when he called. The Good Shepherd of the sheep thought of other flocks which he called His and which one day could be made into one flock with one Shepherd.

The fold, of course, has its uses, but the general tendency of language to give the name of an assembly, congregation, or society to the place in which it meets, has many illustrations. When we use the word synagogue, we think of a building; but the synagogue was primarily a congregation, a meeting, the name of which came to be applied to the place in which it met, so that the original and true meaning of the word has been misapplied to a building. The same of course is true of words like school and college. Most English people when they see the word college, think of some building. But this is not the true meaning of the word. A college, for instance at Oxford or Cambridge, is usually a Society of fellows and scholars, whose meeting-place generally was at first called a hall; now it is called a college.

The word 'Church', which only describes the flock, the society of Christian people, is commonly applied to the buildings in this country where the Church meets, and is also often applied to the human organization which also may be compared to the fold. The Greek word '*ecclesia*' was a translation of the Jewish word for synagogue, and meant a group of people meeting together. This word is not preserved in the English word 'Church', which is derived from the Greek word '*Kurios*' but is recognized immediately in the French word '*Eglise*'. The Church of Christ, however much the name is applied to buildings, institutions, and ecclesiastical organizations, in reality is always the flock of the Good Shepherd, and only in a secondary sense the fold which shelters it.

The word 'Church' (*Ecclesia*) in the New Testament is used

in two senses. It is applied to local communities, as for instance the Church of Corinth, but it is also used as the description of the whole body of Christians on earth and in Heaven, the Church Militant and the Church Triumphant. This conception of the Catholic Church is vividly expressed in St Paul's Epistles to the Ephesians and Colossians. Paul thinks of the Body of Christ and its building up as something that will only be finally accomplished in the future. 'Till we all come in the unity of the faith, and of the knowledge of the Son of God, a perfect man, unto the measure of the stature of the fulness of Christ'.[1] 'The church, which is his body, the fulness of him that filleth all in all.'[2] Though opinions differ, this passage seems to speak not of the adult individual but of the adult corporation. Through divisions, troubles and difficulties, the Church of Christ is growing through the centuries from the infant state that Paul found, for instance in the Corinthian Church, to the full stature of Christ Himself. The catholic Church is to be realized in the future. May we not hope and work to that end. It will emerge triumphant notwithstanding its present-day divisions and other childish crudities.

It is not to be wondered that imperfections and weaknesses are to be found through the centuries in the growing Church. When we say 'I believe in the holy catholic Church' we think of the flock of Christ, of those who have overcome and those who are still fighting:

> *One family we dwell in Him,*
>   *One Church, above, beneath,*
> *Though now divided by the stream,*
>   *The narrow stream of death:*
> *One army of the living God,*
>   *To His command we bow,*
> *Part of His Host have crossed the flood,*
>   *And part are crossing now.*

Confusion often arises by the different uses of the same word '*ecclesia*', which describes either a local congregation or the

---

[1] Ephesians 4:13     [2] ibid., 1:23.

Catholic Church. It was in the sense of the Universal Church that the Bishop of Durham recently said that the word could not be used of a body like the Methodist Denomination. I do not object to this statement. Indeed, it was not until 1897 that we used the word 'Church'; before then we were described as the Society of the People called Methodists. And I agree with my friend Dr Wiseman, who often told me that he regarded the change of name as a mistake. Anyhow we never said, 'I believe in the Holy Methodist Church', but always in the 'Holy Catholic Church'; and this because we do not believe in the identification of the flock of the Good Shepherd with any fold or organization of human structure. So the Bishop of Durham perhaps would hardly object, if words are to be used accurately rather than politely, if one doubts the right of Anglicans to call themselves in any exclusive sense the Catholic Church. As the situation is today, there are many folds, but always one flock. The true believers in Jesus Christ who live in fellowship with His people are the True Church.

In what sense is the Church to be called visible? Only literally in its potentiality, because the whole Church on earth cannot be visualized. The Church becomes visible in local congregations, in the worship and the fellowship of followers of Christ. And any fellowship, however small, which is created by the presence of Christ, is really the Catholic Church. It is capable of singing together with the whole Church Militant and Triumphant:

> *Therefore with angels and archangels: And with all the company of heaven,*
> *We laud and magnify Thy glorious name: evermore praising Thee and saying,*
> *Holy, holy, holy: Lord God of hosts.*
> *Heaven and earth are full of Thy glory: Glory be to Thee O Lord most high.*

Many Protestants criticize the Roman claim that the Church is the Kingdom of Christ on earth. So far as the Church is not identified with any particular fold, I question this criticism.

It is most strongly made by those who think that the Kingdom of God merely signifies the reign of God and not the Realm. But as we have seen earlier, it is impossible to think of the rule of the monarch unless he has a realm in which to reign. Hence it seems reasonable to say that the people who acknowledge, and notwithstanding with more or less imperfection, obey, their King, are none other than the realm in which He reigns. One can understand the disinclination of Christian people to apply the term realm or Kingdom of God to any Church either past or present, on account of the many mundane aspects of its life. At some times and places the Church of God has far from shown the marks of a realm ruled by Jesus Christ. But if the Kingdom of God is a Kingdom on earth and is in any sense visible, it is obvious that it must be looked for amongst the people who profess to be the subjects of Christ.

We are told by the critics of this view that the words '*Ecclesia*' and '*Basileia*' are never identified in the New Testament; but does this really matter? If the people of God, His subjects, are found in His Church and found there in an organized form and profess themselves to be subject to His Rule, what is this but to say, if the word '*Basileia*' can ever be translated as Realm, as we see it can, that this is the Kingdom of God on earth.

This of course does not mean that it is the Kingdom of God fully developed; but it does mean that that Kingdom which Jesus said 'has now come upon you' is still here in the subjects of Christ.

Much depends on whether the Kingdom of God is at hand, or whether it has actually arrived. As Dr Dodd's *Realized Eschatology* is accepted in these pages, there must be some continuum on earth of the Kingdom of God which has come. Where can it be found except in the Church, the community which acknowledges the reign of Christ on earth, and strives to extend His Kingdom?

Does anyone believe that the Kingdom disappeared when Jesus disappeared from sight, and can only be realized when He comes again? The whole history of Christianity, as described in the Acts of the Apostles, and as interpreted by the fourth Evangelist, contradicts any such assumption. If this is so, the Rule of God on Earth implies a realm in which He rules. As His subjects are to be found in organized form, nowhere else than in His Church—His *Ecclesia*—there can be no doubt that the English word 'Kingdom' means that this is the realm of Christ. And since it is unquestionable that at least in its secondary meaning the Greek word '*Basileia*' is often translated 'realm', it may well be concluded that it is legitimate to call the organizations in which the subjects of Christ give Him obedience and treat Him as King, the Kingdom of Christ, that is, the Kingdom of God on earth.

It is important to realize the continuity of the Church of Christ with that Kingdom of God which Jesus declared had actually arrived.

It must never be forgotten, whenever the Church, that is to say the flock of the Good Shepherd, is thought of as the Kingdom of God on earth, that as in other kingdoms there are very unsatisfactory subjects. It has sometimes been said that the Church is for sinners only and this no doubt is true. Redeemed through the mercy of God, as the members of His family are, the best of them are most conscious of their imperfections. The claim often made by those outside the Church that Christians are inconsistent with their profession is undoubtedly true. If it be thought that their profession means that they are Christ-like, the most that can be said of the best of them (and the Saints are most ready to say it) is that they always pray: 'God be merciful to us, Sinners.' But with all the disloyalties which grieve them, and which create moods of penitence, they do accept the Kingship of Jesus and strive to obey Him. It is easy enough to be consistent with your standard if your standard is low enough. With all its faults there can be no doubt that the society in which the Kingship of Christ is acknowledged and always has been, more than any other organization, is the Light of the World and the Salt of the Earth.

Two names of Christian sects describe as well as any I can

think of, the interior and exterior life of the Holy Catholic Church: the Society of Friends, and the Salvation Army. The inner life, which in the Creeds is called the Communion of the Saints, is that of the Society of the Friends of Jesus—because it is in their relation to the Christ who lives in their midst that their friendship consists. Fellowship with Him creates fellowship one with another. The Church is never a mere man-made club with certain common interests, but always the flock of the Good Shepherd, created and kept in being through His presence, and Leadership. It is also an army set in the world to be the instrument in the extension of the Kingdom of Christ which, when He has completely won, as St Paul says, He will deliver up to the Father that God may be All in All. Every Christian is, as it were, a conscripted soldier of Christ. In the later Chapters the Militant service of the Church will be treated.

How does the Church do its work in the world? By witness. Christians, both as individuals and as a corporate body, are the instruments of Christ in extending His Kingdom; that is in carrying on His work to destroy the Devil and all his works. The corporate witness of the Church is made through her Sacraments, which are not only a witness to the world, but the means of the deepest unification of all Christian people. While it is true that various opinions of the meaning of the two universal Sacraments of Baptism and the Lord's Supper have often caused divisions and controversies, it is also true that, however administered, they are, with negligible exceptions, the witness of the Church to the world. While in Apostolic times Baptism was the universal symbol of initiation into the Church, it was natural, as today in heathen countries, for it to be normally given to adult converts, either from Judaism or Heathenism. There seem to have been isolated cases of infant baptism even in the first century, but the problem of the relation of children to the Church became acute later; and the notion of some people today that the little child whom Jesus set in the midst should be excluded from His Church, is one that could not be sustained in the early years of Christianity. It may be that the baptism of infants is in some sense prophetic, and only fully effective when the child grows up and consciously submits itself to Christ. Nothing can be more important than the bringing of the lambs into the fold. But most of all, the Holy Eucharist both shows forth to the world the death of our Lord, till He come, and perpetually proclaims to all men the complete reliance of Christian people upon His redeeming work. It also gives spiritual food and nourishment to the followers of the Saviour, who confess in their very eating of that bread and drinking of that wine, that their spiritual life would fade and die without the food, the Bread of Life, with which Christ feeds His people. This great devotion, central in the life of the Christian Church, practised in different ways through nearly twenty centuries, is so rich in meaning and so expressive of the deepest truths of Christianity, that its observance and practice is central in the Worship of God's people.

But the chief influence which the Church of Christ has had on the world, great as its corporate devotions have been, has been the higher life and morality of its people. In early Christianity the plain superiority of the Christian life over that of pagan peoples was the greatest factor in its successful evangelization of the world. Not only by the many martyrdoms which proved the triumphant Faith, but by their spirit of forgiveness of injuries, and purity of life, they convinced their contemporaries that they had a secret possessed by none other. There have, it is true, been periods in the history of all Christian institutions when the Saviour has been parodied by His followers, but the truth has been made visible where Christian conduct has been conscientiously practised, as it has been in all ages, notwithstanding glaring exceptions. It is by the fruits of the Spirit that the greatest Christian victories have been won, and the Kingdom of Christ extended.

The divisions of Christianity are perhaps the most serious obstacle to the work of the Church in the world. If only today the Christian people could realize that the Flock of Christ is a Society of Friends, made friends not by mere common denominational interests, but by fellowship with Christ, which involves fellowship one with another, we should reach the central uniting realities of Christianity. I have attended many conferences to discuss methods for the unification of Christian people, and while they have often been edifying and helpful, they have too often, it seems to me, been concerned with the unification of the folds, rather than with the unity of the Flock. External differences have been more conspicuously discussed than the interior unity which is to be found amongst all people who really love the Saviour. I am convinced that it is more important to begin at the centre than at the circumference. Indeed, an incident in my early ministry brought home to me the possibilities of the union of Christian people, more than any of the Conferences dealing with externals ever have done. One day I visited an old woman in my congregation. She told me how interested she had been in something that I had said about Christian Fellowship in my sermon on the previous Sunday morning. A woman of some seventy years of age in the year 1900, she said: 'I remembered my own girlhood. At the age of sixteen, I was converted and was very happy. I spent my time singing all the day. One morning, in the village where I lived, I had to go to the village pump as usual to get water for the house. It was a bright and beautiful spring morning and so I sang because my heart was full of joy:

> *My God, I am Thine,*
> *What a comfort Divine,*
> *What a blessing to know that my Jesus is mine!*

and went on singing the hymn until I came to the pump. But there was another woman there, a grim-looking person, who belonged, I knew, to a Particular Baptist Church (that is to say one of the few remaining churches of the severe and exclusive Calvinistic type), and she looked very shocked; but I thought I had better go on singing, so I continued:

> *My Jesus to know,*
> *And to feel His blood flow,*
> *'Tis life everlasting, 'tis Heaven below.*

And then I noticed another girl, an Irish girl, newly come to the village, on her way to the pump. And I thought, "She is Irish, she may be a Roman Catholic". So when she came I sang again, "My Jesus to know...". Both of them evidently thought I was rather mad, and asked me what was the matter with me. I told them nothing was the matter, I was so happy because of the love of Jesus, and I told them all about my conversion, and about Jesus and His love. Then to my great surprise the Catholic girl crossed herself and began to talk about the Precious Blood of Christ and about her love for Jesus, and a smile illuminated even the gloomy face of the Calvinistic woman, and she too talked about the love of Jesus, and her hope that she might be one of the elect. And we all became very happy talking about Jesus, and what He meant to us. I forgot that I was a Methodist, and the others forgot the distinctions of denomination, but we had true Fellowship one with another because of the Love that breaks down the barriers erected by a separated fold.'

Surely it is here in the central experience of people who realize that the Cross of Christ breaks down middle walls of partition, and makes us one. But the Fellowship in Jesus Christ, sweet and strong as it may be, is not all. The Church of Christ is not only a Society of Friends but also a Salvation Army—of that I write in the last chapter of this book.

PART THREE

# THE MODERN SITUATION AND EVANGELISM

CHAPTER NINE

## THEN AND NOW

*Saviour, we know Thou art*
*In every age the same:*
*Now, Lord, in ours exert*
*The virtue of Thy name;*
*And daily, through Thy word, increase*
*Thy blood-besprinkled witnesses.*

*Thy people, saved below,*
*From every sinful stain,*
*Shall multiply and grow,*
*If Thy command ordain;*
*And one into a thousand rise,*
*And spread Thy praise through earth and skies.*

THE WORDS of a man born in 1870, who has experienced two world wars and a Social Revolution, must seem to a modern man to express the thoughts of an antediluvian; but one whose memory goes back into the past has at least the advantage, however much he is dazzled and uncertain in his vision of the present, of possessing a vivid and experienced view of an earlier age. If one adds but a decade or two to a life beginning in 1870, the contrast between the past and the present becomes even more startling. The tremendous changes of the last century have been as rapid and complete as that of a millenium. People living in the earlier part of the nineteenth century, before the introduction of steam locomotion on land and sea, in many ways were nearer to the people of the Roman Empire, than to those of 1950. But even I, looking back into my own past life, visualize a world very different to that of the present day. For instance, I remember travelling from a village to a railway station some ten miles away in what was then called a 'fly', which nearly did the journey in an hour. The rapidity of that fly is not very impressive in a day when aeroplanes can travel at over 700 miles an hour. I remember well the excitement (when I was a boy) of the town of Reading when the first electric arc lamps came into being. Ten years later, in my early twenties, I remember seeing one of the first motor-cars which broke down in the streets of Leicester, and the crowds of people who cheered when horses were brought to drag it away, and the confident laughter of the sceptics who said: 'I told you they would always break down.' I remember, too, the incredulity of people who said that they knew that air travel was impossible, and were really angry when Bleriot crossed the Channel. And so one might go on to speak of the changes of the last eighty years. Many things have happened that another age would have called miracles. The telephone, the cinema, the wonders of wireless and television, which even now to a non-scientific mind seem almost magical.

Progress in the application of science to the uses of life has been so rapid that it is difficult for anyone in our times to realize the amazing revolution through which we have passed and the consequent changes in the thought and outlook of the people. A working man today has luxuries which were not to be found in a palace a century ago. The changed situation is not only in the material life, since material changes have profoundly affected the inner life of human beings.

I shall attempt no analysis of the modern situation, not only because of my incompetence for understanding some of its features, but also because the excellent analysis of Dr Donald Soper in his Presidential address to the Methodist Conference—an address which I hope will find a more permanent form than that of the current newspaper—is much the best account which I know of the modern situation in its relation to the Church and to Evangelism.

The 'lethal indifference' of the modern crowd which, as Dr Soper says, almost breaks the heart of open-air Christian propagandists, differs from the more hostile character of the people of 1890. Their hostility was not so much against Christ—indeed one may regard our Lord as a popular character with the people of those days—but it was often fierce against the Church and the representative of the Church. It would not be true to say of those days that Evangelists offered to the people 'something' of which they did not feel the need. They did not question, for instance, the Christian standards of sex morality. Even when men broke Christian laws or disregarded them they knew that they had done wrong and a sense of guilt was not difficult to arouse. The doubts of today which Dr Soper records as to the supremacy of Jesus found no very vocal expression. The crowds of the last century were far too British in sentiment to be moved by Hindu or other Eastern religions. The scientific training of people and the influence of two world wars upon their minds was non-existent at the earlier date. Communism in its Russian form obviously, was unheard of, though the people, many of whom suffered from economic and social causes, were full of social aspirations, but in England those aspirations were often perhaps generally of a Christian rather than an atheistic source. The people felt that if only the Churches obeyed Jesus Christ, social inequalities would vanish. The belief in hell and heaven, though perhaps a diminishing belief, was still held in common by the people inside and the people outside the Churches. War, which so overshadows the minds of the people of today with their bitter memories, and the prospects of atomic warfare of incredible horror, had no influence whatever on the minds of the people then. Not only Christian people, but rationalists like Buckle regarded future war among civilized people as a practical impossibility. Whereas people of that day would have been completely incredulous if anyone had pictured to them the aeroplane, the radio or television, or many other scientific discoveries and implementations, it is hardly an exaggeration to say that war between civilized Western peoples would have seemed equally incredible. It was an age in which everyone believed in progress. The theory of evolution which at first caused trouble amongst the orthodox was increasingly accepted by ordinary people at the end of the nineteenth century and in many pulpits was beginning to be regarded as an evidence for progress toward

> That one far-off divine event
> To which the whole creation moves.

### (II) DR SOPER'S ANALYSIS WITH MY COMMENTS

Of the three overtowering facts to which Dr Soper calls our attention, the first—war and peace—has through the nation's bitter experience become a problem of first importance.

(a) The Church, he argues, must make no compromise with war. He does not define his meaning in this sentence, but he is undoubtedly right in claiming that the followers of the Prince of Peace must hate war and seek peace and ensue it. Different opinions are held and are likely to be maintained as to how peace is best to be assured.

The charge sometimes made by pacifist critics of the Church that the Church is little better than a society of war-mongers is extravagant and even preposterous. That historical instances can be quoted of the Church's use of war for its own temporal advantage both in Catholic and Protestant communities is no doubt true. Whether we think of the Crusades or the disgraceful wars of the Renaissance such as those of Pope Pius II or perhaps even of the Old Testament fury of the Cromwellians, we have to acknowledge that the ideals of the Prince of Peace were set aside. But on the whole, throughout the last 2000 years, the Church much more than any other organization has stood for peace, and even when she has not practised it she has not failed to preach it, and there are many instances—one can find them in the historical plays of Shakespeare—of the fact that the conscience of the Church was on the side of peace and that breaches of peace needed argument, sometimes it is true very casuistical, for their defence. When the Pope refused in 1914 to bless the Austrians in their warfare and said, 'I bless peace not war', he gave a brave and true expression of the Christian conscience. If ever peace is to be established on the earth the organization most capable and most likely to establish it is the Church of Christ. If that great 'International' could be really united and its grievous and un-Christlike divisions annihilated, the prospect of peace amongst the nations would be much brighter.

At the same time it must not be forgotten that wars in a true sense are judgements of God. Whatsoever the nations sow that must they also reap. Modern wars were sown long ago, sometimes even in past centuries in the hatreds, jealousies, vows of vengeance, lusts, ambitions, greed—which seeds must come to harvest. Sometimes wars fall upon us with the sudden force of a terrible storm or a crashing avalanche. They are almost like the forces of Nature. The attitude of the individual Christian to such wars when they come will always be determined by his own conscience. The principal duty of the Church today is to create the spirit of love and fellowship, the practice of the precepts of the Sermon on the Mount through the realization that all men of all nations are potentially the children of the heavenly Father.

Our attitude toward those whom we call enemies and who think of us as enemies requires a concentration of our mind on the fact that all children of the heavenly Father are to be treated by us as brothers. The creation by action of the spirit of charity which the Church of all institutions can most readily and most naturally create, as it becomes the general practice of the Church, ensures a positive spirit of unity which will certainly make for peace, however apparently irrelevant such actions may seem toward great national issues. The followers of the Prince of Peace are under perpetual obligation to do their utmost to prevent political and international action in our own day which will produce, with the inevitable sequence of harvest from seed, the catastrophe of war.

The practice of the Church in this as in most other things has been lower than her ideals. But the ideal has never been lost. The bright starlight angel ideal has too often been represented by a dingy candle-flame, but the Lord still moves among the candlesticks.[1] It must never be forgotten that the Church is not a

[1] Revelation 1¹³.

company of saints, but of sinners only—sinners being saved.

(b) The second outstanding fact Dr Soper says 'is the concern for human welfare whether organized in the Welfare State or inarticulate'. The contrast between today and half a century ago is that the aspirations, hopes and dreams of 'then' have been in large measure realized 'now'. Some of the apocalyptic visions of 1890–1910, it is true, have not been realized, and never will be so long as human sinfulness remains. But much has been accomplished both by scientists and politicians to bring about the material benefits in which we all share and in which all Christians should rejoice.

'Then' was the day of *Looking Backward*, *Merrie England*, and (before Robert Blatchford made his regrettable crusade against Christianity) *The Clarion*. Strong support for the ideals and principles of these popular publications was to be found in many Christian circles. The contribution of the Churches to the social betterment of England was much greater than many people think. Clear evidence of this fact is to be found in an earlier chapter.[2]

Problems today are created by the materialization of the dreams and hopes of fifty years ago. Success creates its problems as truly as need. Can the hungry soul of men be satisfied with radio, television and cinemas, or even by football pools?

However much we may rejoice in the bettered social conditions of the people, nothing could be worse in Dr Soper's opinion than satisfaction with the purely material life, and he finds a wistful longing amongst them for something higher which Christianity alone can satisfy. People are turning away, he thinks, both from Communist ideology and the promises of scientific benefits. A few years ago eminent representative scientists told us that if we would but let science alone to do its own work it would produce an earthly paradise. While science has done much to enrich life, it must not be forgotten that its power to do evil is also great. Some people claim that its greatest accomplishment is the atomic bomb!

[2] pp. 32ff., *supra*.

(c) The power of politics as the great engine of change is indeed notable. Men seem to believe, Dr Soper tells us, rather in the Omnicompetent State than in the Omnipotent God. This is a great challenge to Christianity. The problem of the Church to influence political action without being a political party or subservient to a political party is one of the most important of the time. The dis-union of the Churches minimizes tragically the political power of the Church. At the turn of the centuries there was much political movement in the Free Churches: but the fact that the Churches generally speaking were attached to different political parties was a cause of conflict between them. Attachment of the separated Churches to particular political parties hardly exists today and is no longer a cause of friction.

Politicians, Dr Soper truly says, have joined with parsons in appealing for a spiritual revival. The true Welfare State is utterly dependent on this. 'It is one thing to inspire a revolution with fervour, another to supply moral energy to maintain it.' 'After years of open-air work I know of no other claim in the name of Jesus which makes a more immediate appeal to the outsider' than this claim that he is necessary to the Welfare State since the outsider knows that the claim is true. If people are not turning to Christ they are turning away from His competitors. 'Communism can only maintain its ideals by renouncing its ideology. Christianity can only reach its ideals by practising its teaching.'

(d) Christianity properly understood and applied is entirely relevant to the situation. That relevancy is expressed by Dr Soper in the following important words:

'The lessons we draw from all this are by no means destructive of the Gospel. I assert that all these render the Gospel infinitely more relevant. The answer to this secular state with its terrific power is not individual piety, which now is often exposed to overwhelming odds, and moreover is often nothing more or better than the image cast upon the private screen of our personal behaviour of the sort of society in which we live, but the Kingdom of God which Jesus bids us seek first and against which the gates of Hell shall not prevail. For only when our personal behaviour reflects the Kingdom of God is our piety genuine and invincible.

'The might of governments must be opposed or transformed or sustained by the Church; Christians unorganized and divided one from another will not suffice; secular society can only be outmatched by the Divine Society, but that Divine Society can command illimitable resources. *That is why reunion is not only desirable but imperative*, and, without bitterness, let me add, that is why Christian sects which offer to their devotees nothing more than an individual experience are intolerable. Our only safety is in the Body of Christ.

'Need I stress the other and more obvious need for a Christian Church to give the broad outline and pattern of political action without itself becoming a political party? Governments are superb and amazingly efficient servants, they are impermissible as masters; for, as our Lord said, the servant knoweth not what his Lord doeth. "The Son of Man hath power on earth"—only when that Son of Man is Jesus. Only when Jesus is Master and Lord can we rest assured that his power will be used for blessing and not for cursing.'

This does not mean that piety is of no account, but it does mean that piety merely concerned with a man's deliverance from his own sins is not genuine Christian piety. Jesus came to make a new world as well as to make new men. The object of these pages is to relate the fundamental fact of the Old Evangelist, that Jesus came into the world to save sinners, with the older Gospel of Jesus, the Good News that the Kingdom of God has already come and that our first duty is to change our minds and seek it. We must make a fresh start; we must become as little children that we may participate in the new world—the Kingdom of Christ on earth.

As we compare 'then' and 'now' we shall deal in the next chapter with changes in the Church which create difficulties for the modern evangelist which did not exist then.

## (III) THEN AND NOW ILLUSTRATED

But one change, generally recognized as an improvement, the quickening of the social conscience of the Church, may be noted here. The individualism of the old evangelical appeal rose from the emphasis based on individual sin and individual salvation. Sometimes this resulted in a regrettable morbidity, but generally the concentration of the mind upon the questions of personal salvation and relation of the soul to God was stressed out of proportion to the social obligations of Christian men; although, of course, charity to the needy and kindness to others were virtues inculcated and practised by Christian people. There was little sense of the social obligation of Christians, especially of Wesleyans, to influence political life or to fight against the social evils which made righteousness almost impossible for great masses of their fellow citizens. People little thought that negligence in social activity was a sin against God. The awakening of the social conscience of the Church has been a marked feature amongst evangelicals in recent years. A danger, however, of forgetting that a humble walk with God is necessary for the permanent performance of justice and the love of mercy must not be overlooked. To walk humbly with God is not just the tag end of the great words of the prophet Micah but the essential fact in his answer to the question: 'What does God require of thee but to do justly, to love mercy, and to walk humbly with thy God?'

The change from 'then' to 'now', increasingly plain, is the alienation of the masses of the people of England from the Church. In my youth the galleries of our churches and chapels, in great centres of population, were crowded with young people. Today, in most places, they are not even opened. In my youth, we always calculated that the number of Methodists in a particular church was two or three times as great as the membership of the church. Today it is a rare thing to find a congregation as large as the membership. In the time of the Forward Movement described in an earlier chapter, our churches were often crowded with people, outsiders, strangers as we called them. Today, in most Methodist churches, the stranger is a *rara avis* whose presence is noted and talked about by the normal members of the congregation as exceptional. The indifference of the multitudes of English people to the very existence of the Church is a humiliating fact which must be acknowledged. The proportion of the church-going population to the population of England seems to be very low, though it may be claimed that the methods of calculating this are not very satisfactory. Yet, the people who say that England is a Pagan country today are certainly not without evidence for this statement. The sooner we realize that the Church must regard itself as a Missionary organization in a neo-pagan country, the better it will be for us.

CHAPTER TEN

# MODERN DIFFICULTIES FOR EVANGELISTS

*To serve the present age*
*My calling to fulfil*
*Oh may it all my power engage*
*To do my Master's will.*

### THE EFFECT OF CHURCH CHANGES ON EVANGELISM

DR SOPER as the preceding chapter shows gave special attention to the modern situation which confronts the Church of Christ. In the following chapters I shall emphasize rather the relation of the Church to the modern situation, not forgetting his valuable words on the relevance of the Gospel.

We must face facts. I have pointed out earlier that in my experience, especially in recent times, the Fundamentalist has been the most immediately effective evangelistic appeal, but whatever are the immediate results it is increasingly impossible for people to blind themselves to facts as the Fundamentalists do. There can be no future for the adherence to a literal interpretation of the Bible without any understanding that the Bible is not a book but a library of many books. God reveals Himself in many ways, through myth and poetry as well as through law and history. The contrasts outlined in the previous chapter, between our own days and the past days when the old evangelical appeal was successful, cannot be ignored. If the success of evangelical appeal today is slower to those who try to face all the facts, it is more sure. Nothing is sadder than the total disintegration of the faith of people which has been based upon views of religion promulgated by men who, because of some really exploded theory, blind their minds to ascertained truth. Unfortunately the blind, or those who do not wish to see, love to be led by the blind. Few books are more moving and pathetic than Philip Gosse's *Father and Son*, which shows the way in which the author's father, a brilliant scientist and geologist, employs very eccentric devices to harmonize his inherited theory of the Book of Genesis with his own geological discoveries. As we shall see presently, there is no more essential fact in the religion of Jesus Christ than that His Kingdom is a Kingdom of Truth.

Of the contrasts between 'then' and 'now' in the Church itself I will set down here what seem to me to be the most important:

(a) The authority of the Bible.
(b) The secularization of Sunday.
(c) The decay of Puritanism.
(d) The fear of hell and judgement.

## (A) THE AUTHORITY OF THE BIBLE

Probably the greatest loss to the evangelist in our own time is the discredit into which the Bible as an infallible source of reference has fallen through the criticism of modern scholars. The alternative to the man in the street often seems to be either the acceptance of the Fundamentalist conception of its literal truth or rejection. In point of fact, modern scholarship has really made the Bible a more intelligible book, but the values of this scholarship have not yet filtered into the popular mind. Is it not an obligation of the Christian scholars who have destroyed the traditional conception of the Bible to so restore it as to make the hope of the greatest pioneer of such scholarship, Erasmus, come true?

'For I utterly dissent', he wrote, 'from those who are unwilling that the sacred Scriptures should be read by the unlearned, translated into their vulgar tongue, as though Christ had taught such subtleties that they can scarcely be understood even by a few theologians, or as though the strength of the Christian religion consisted in men's ignorance of it. . . . I long that the husbandman should sing portions of them to himself as he follows the plough, that the weaver should hum them to the tune of his shuttle, that the traveller should beguile with their stories the tedium of his journey.'

Speaking for myself, I have never more realized that the Bible contains the word of the living God, though accepting much that modern scholars have taught me, than I do today. But the fact that it is difficult to appeal to the Bible as an authoritative book in modern evangelism is of such outstanding moment that nothing matters more than its popularization in the truer setting which has been given to it. I have sometimes wondered whether a council of biblical experts on the one hand and practical evangelists on the other could not together solve a problem of such immense importance. It were indeed a tragedy if, after rejecting the infallible interpretation of the Roman Church, the man to whom Protestantism gave an open Bible should be dependent not on his own reading but upon a so-called infallible(?) judgement of experts of whom it may be said: 'When doctors differ who shall then agree?'

For such movements as the 'Bible Speaks Today' of the Bible Society we cannot but be too thankful, but they will be futile unless attention is given to the new interpretation made necessary by modern research and scholarship.

### (B) THE SECULARIZATION OF SUNDAY

The gradual secularization of Sunday is a serious hindrance to the evangelist. Although the Puritan Sabbath cannot be restored, because its Old Testament basis is sub-Christian, the necessity of regular worship is of great importance. The worship of God, no doubt, can be rendered anywhere and at any time as food can be taken at any time for the nourishment of the body; but regularity of meals is desirable in both cases. Though regular private devotion is essential to the Christian life it is hardly more important than regular corporate devotion. The spiritual family, like the natural family, needs regular meals. The separation of Sunday from the other days of the week regularizes times of devotion, without which it would indeed be difficult to feed the corporate life of the Christian Church.

The connexion of Sunday with regular worship is of vital importance because evangelism itself, if unrooted in worship and divorced from it, is hopelessly weakened. Nothing was more conspicuous in the first decade, the greatest days of the Evangelical Revival, than the worship, even the eucharistic worship, of the first followers of the Wesleys.

### (c) THE DECAY OF PURITANISM

I should be the last man to deny the immense contribution Puritanism made to our national and religious life. The stress of seriousness, even though sometimes grim, was an essential factor in the creation and development of the British character. Here, however, I am thinking of the degenerate Puritanism of my early years which had become a religion of taboos and trifles. The ideal character of those days, seems to have been almost entirely negative. A man's goodness was calculated by what he did not do, rather than by what he did. Not only was he to keep the negative Commandments, but if he was to express the Puritan ideal he had to abstain from a number of things which were categorically defined as worldliness. In point of fact, the parallel between Puritanism of that period and the Phariseeism of the first century is very close. The taboos of the period condemned as worldly many perfectly innocent practices, especially in the realm of amusements and certain forms of cultural life. The use of the theatre, card-playing, dancing and other like practices were prohibited as actually sinful. Dr W. E. Sangster in his widely read sermon, *This England*, claims that the Church has no objection to the stage but stands for its purification. In my youth a Methodist minister who made such a statement would certainly have been subjected to discipline instead of being elected to the chair of the Methodist Conference.

Dancing was regarded as a quick though gay route to the Devil. A pack of cards was called the 'Devil's Bible'. The demand for the observance of these rigid Puritan taboos was common in the pulpit of the day though even then attempts, not a little hypocritical, were made to evade them. For instance,

I knew people who, while they thought it wicked to use playing-cards, would make a pack with numbers from one to thirteen written on them and play such games as Patience with them. The game of whist was regarded as a game for the wicked. A well-known minister, a friend of mine, of strict Methodist training, told me that an aunt of his who prided herself upon her Methodism always said whist was a very wicked game, but taught him bezique, which she regarded, for some unaccountable reason, as a sacred rite. Let me set down a few instances in my own experience. My father told me that when he was a young man he was seriously criticized in an official Methodist meeting for playing the worldly game of chess. My maternal grandfather, a solicitor, who was a local preacher, was severely rebuked for quoting secular literature in the pulpit. The secular author was William Shakespeare and the quotation: 'The quality of mercy is not strained'! Today these unlovely remnants of Puritanism have been almost entirely swept away. It must be admitted however that there is loss as well as gain in such changes. We have learned in our own days that there is much more good in bad people than our fathers thought, and much more bad in good. The clear dichotomy between good and bad, the Church and the world, unquestionably made evangelical appeal easier. We leave it today to our Lord to separate the sheep from the goats, as our fathers did not.

The loss today of the decadent Puritanism of sixty years ago, which still lingers among out-of-date people in out-of-way places, cannot be regretted. A negative religion of taboos and morbid self-examination was certainly not the religion of Jesus Christ. The torture of a rich and imaginative mind, like that of John Bunyan, depicted in his great confessional book *Grace Abounding*, verges on insanity. The haunting sense of guilt which so plagued that good man who exaggerated mere peccadilloes into heinous sins was unhealthy, however glorious may have been his issue out of all his afflictions in his acceptance of the illuminating experience he had of the grace of God. He, like Luther before him, realized with exultant joy that

Jesus loved *him*, not only loved Paul and Peter, but loved *him*, John Bunyan. Sir Oliver Lodge, a few years ago shocked the orthodox world by saying that the people of this age 'no longer worry about sin': that should certainly be the attitude of Christian people who are exhorted by St Paul to leave the things that are behind and to press forward. A great Protestant, the notable hymn-writer, Tersteegen, in his day made a very necessary protest:

'Do not think about sin, at least not deliberately. The thought often arouses temptation. Fixed and constant gazing at our sins and temptations makes us little of courage and little of faith. Or are you afraid that so many sins and strong temptations may arise, that Jesus will not be able to help you any more? Foolish creature! Regard your sins and all that works in you against your will, as something that does not concern you: leave the horror there; it is not worth your remembrance and attention. Experience teaches us that great temptations are often overcome by simply forgetting them. Reflect that you have something else to do in the world than always to think about sin. God and His Presence must be the principal business of your heart. If it again seizes hold of you, how miserable, corrupt, and full of sin you are, then say, "I know that full well, but just now I have no time to think about it".'

Few people have been happier than the early Methodists in their sense of forgiveness of sins, but even with them there were moments of reaction and morbidity. I have heard from more sources than one, and I have no doubt that the saying is true, though I have never been able to verify it in his works, that John Wesley was compelled to change his instructions to his early Bands, small groups of Methodists who met together in the early days to confess their sins to each other. The frank confession of their sins and thoughts about them tended to morbidity, with the consequence that he told his people to confess not their sins, but their Saviour.

These people, who discovered to their great joy the pardoning grace of the heavenly Father, sometimes tended to appropriate the Father to themselves without remembering His family, and

## MODERN DIFFICULTIES FOR EVANGELISTS 119

failed to develop Wesley's doctrine of Perfect Love, probably because they did not realize sufficiently explicitly our Saviour's proclamation of the Kingdom of God as a family of love. The obsession with the sense of sin tended to create, especially through their desire to flee from the wrath of God, an individualism which dominated too much the children of the Evangelical Revival when their great leader was taken away from them. The individual desire to flee from the wrath to come and to be saved from their sins, conceived out of relation to the corporate implications of our Lord's good news that the Kingdom of God had come, degenerated into an individualism which, in my early days, though marked often with great piety and devotion, did tend to express itself in the taboos and negations of an earlier Puritanism.

The Christian life does not consist in inaction, but in activity. Goodness does not consist in not doing this and that and the other, but in doing what is good. The people who are always stressing the sinlessness of Christ as if it were the chief fact of His character are really mistaken, as this is the least thing we claim for Him. Jesus was and is the Light of the World. He gladdens and brightens everything that he touches.

> *Christ, whose glory fills the skies,*
> *Christ, the true, the only Light,*
> *Son of Righteousness, arise,*
> *Triumph o'er the shades of night.—*

These are great words, truly descriptive of the Saviour. It is extraordinary how some pious people imagine that to do nothing wrong, or even doubtful, is the ideal of life. They should be reminded that Christ said to the people who do nothing that they should go away into everlasting punishment. Those who did it not to one of the least of His children were damned, not for doing evil, but for doing nothing. An incidence in my own experience illustrates what I mean. Into a very happy class of newly converted men, full of the sense of victory over sin in themselves through the grace of Jesus Christ, a stranger entered one day, a melancholy-looking person, who sat at the back of the room and listened with a rather sardonic smile upon his face to the happy testimonies of the members of the class. Suddenly he said: 'May I speak, sir?' 'Certainly', I replied. Then he said: 'I do not drink, I do not smoke, I do not go to theatres, I do not dance, I do not even go to secular concerts, I do not play cricket, I do not play football, I do not even go to cricket and football matches, I do not eat meat, neither beef, mutton, nor pork!' He looked very pleased with himself, but I could not help saying: 'My friend, you have told us what you do not do; will you tell us what you do do?' And he could not. The foolish man thought he was saved for doing nothing.

This negative attitude is a pernicious and degenerate form of Christianity. Its taboos are silly, irritating, and essentially Pharisaic. The Church should shake them off. A good man is not a man who is merely harmless, but a man who does good things, who illuminates and brightens the world with his life and witness, who seeks not so much to save his own soul as to save the souls of other people, and their bodies. Christianity enriches humanity; it is a gain to the Church to rid itself of the dregs of an outworn individualistic piety, and to declare the gospel, the good news, the gospel of forgiveness of sins, not only of the forgiveness of sins, but the whole gospel, the gospel of the risen life and of the redeemed community, the gospel which Jesus taught of the Kingdom of God here on earth, the first thing which men must seek—the gospel, not only of new men, but of a new world. A positive, not a negative, gospel, is the need of today.

### (D) THE FEAR OF HELL AND JUDGEMENT

Many of the weapons of the old evangelism are useless in this age of the atom bomb, but is the appeal to fear entirely to be discarded? We cannot, of course, appeal to the fear of Hell, the nightmare form of which appeals to no sensible person today; but it must never be forgotten that the judgement of God is a fact to which it is foolish to close our eyes. St Paul, though the word 'Hell' never occurs in his writings, did appeal to God's historical judgements on the pagan world—and is there any more terrifying passage in literature than that in which he says that the reprobate mind falls upon the people who ignore God. Great historians,[1] as I have already written, especially perhaps Professor Butterfield, have pointed out with great clarity how catastrophic wars and national disasters are the plain results of sin, of lust, pride, ambition, greed, and the spirit of revenge. Though there is no fear of hell today amongst the people of this country they are continually shadowed by the fear of war and atomic weapons. Until Perfect Love casts out fear, fear must always affect multitudes of people. The time can never come when the words of Jesus himself, 'Repent or ye shall all likewise perish', can be dismissed from our minds. The appeal to fear whenever made is, and ought to be, entirely subordinate as it was in the teaching of Jesus. His was the good news that swept away many of the fears of the world, that God, who was expected to come in judgement, had actually come in infinite mercy.

[1] See p. 80, *supra*.

CHAPTER ELEVEN

# THE CHRISTIAN ANSWER TO THE MODERN CHALLENGE

> *Surrounded by a host of foes,*
>   *Stormed by a host of foes within,*
> *Nor swift to flee, nor strong to oppose,*
>   *Single, against hell, earth and sin,*
> *Single, yet undismayed I am:*
> *I dare believe in Jesu's name.*
>
> *What tho' a thousand hosts engage,*
>   *A thousand worlds, my soul to shake?*
> *I have a shield shall quell their rage,*
>   *And drive the alien armies back;*
> *Portray'd it bears a bleeding Lamb:*
> *I dare believe in Jesu's name.*

A SUCCINCT PRESENTATION of the modern challenge to evangelism involves, I fear, some measure of repetition. The special characteristics of our age, as Dr Soper's analysis shows, will certainly make ancient evangelistic methods ineffective. Ours is an age where there is little fear of God and little sense of guilt. The authority of Jesus is challenged in more ways than one, perhaps not very much by other religions, although the voice of Gandhi and his pacifist teaching have demonstrated only the good characteristics of his religion. The Christian standards of morality, especially in relation to sex, generally accepted in the past, are widely challenged today, and though the challenge of Communism has not deeply affected the English mind and seems to be a diminishing force, there can be no doubt that it has offered a solution to people, however unsatisfactory, of certain social evils which Christianity 'truly applied' in the past might have cancelled. But most important of all, ours is an age to which science has made great promises,

## CHRISTIAN ANSWER TO MODERN CHALLENGE 123

many of which have actually been fulfilled. The material prosperity of the Welfare State, although Christianity has had much more to do with this than people realize, is largely the result of scientific technique. What makes for the material good of the people we must all rejoice in. Their life has been enriched in many ways, and while industrialism may be and often does result in a monotonous and mechanical course of existence, the leisure hours of people are enriched by the cinema, television, easy travel and many other things which to a large extent satisfy the mind. The remarkable inventions of our age, so widely shared by all, do divert attention from the Christian appeal, but it is difficult to think that the souls of people can be perpetually satisfied by radio, cinema, and football pools. After all, God has set eternity in our hearts, and a spiritual hunger and wistful longing for something deeper does disturb the mind of the people. Radio listeners in recent years must have heard a good many speeches, most of them not from professing Christians, which regret the moral deterioration of the nation and attribute it to a lack of religion. Amongst such speeches we can count the one by Mr Bertrand Russell, already referred to in Chapter 8.

What then have we to offer the world today? I have no hesitation in saying, 'The Gospel'. By this I mean the full Gospel, the good news that the Kingdom of God is here, and that the Saviour is here to lead his people in the development of it. The good news, too, that Jesus is the Saviour from sin of all men who come to Him. This twofold Gospel, carefully interpreted, and lovingly applied by His followers, can meet the challenge and solve the problems of today. Probably in its fullness it never has been applied yet. In the eighteenth century, for instance, the truth of salvation for every man was gloriously and effectively declared. But the Gospel announced, partially because of the neglect of John Wesley's doctrine of Perfect Love, which his people failed to investigate thoroughly and implement, especially in its social implications, was deficient. In the nineteenth century, on the other hand, the Gospel of the Kingdom of God in its social demands was declared, but in such a way that it degenerated into a mere secularist programme, the deeper truths of evangelical religion having been ignored. We need today the *full* Gospel, the Gospel of individual salvation and the Gospel of the Kingdom of God. Our Lord's priority, 'Seek ye first the Kingdom of God', must not be forgotten. The mere desire of personal salvation, apart from the Kingdom of God, is a one-sided aspiration, but where people repent—change their minds and seek to extend the Kingdom of God and build His city for the good of all mankind—their own salvation will be assured, though its significance will pale in comparison with their quest for a new world, a new world that must have new people in it.

This twofold Gospel has been treated in Chapters 5 to 8 of this book, and here I will only emphasize the two outstanding principles of the Kingdom of God as expounded in the Sermon on the Mount and the teaching of Jesus—Truth and Love.

That it is a Kingdom of Truth is plainly shown in the Sermon on the Mount in two ways—first, by the simple claim that men are to say 'No, no' and 'Yea, yea' and not resort to oaths, because what is required of them everywhere and always is the truth. But chiefly the whole treatment of religion is an emphatic claim for utter sincerity and simplicity. No shams, no pretences, no formalities, no hypocrisies, are tolerable in the righteousness that must exceed that of the Scribes and Pharisees. Our Lord's expression that His Kingdom is the Kingdom of Truth—Reality—is to be found in His memorable interview with Pontius Pilate, who could not understand what Jesus meant. No more impressive scene in history has ever been painted than that interview between the official representative of the great Roman Empire and this humble Galilean, whose dignity and strange witness to this unseen kingdom confounded Pilate as he asked: 'What is truth?' Jesus is the Lord of all truth; His followers have sometimes feared truth when it has been discovered by scientists; some of them still bury their heads in the sand and refuse to acknowledge discoveries and realities which might upset their theories. Christians need fear no truth; they must welcome all, but that does not mean that they need credulously accept the latest scientific nostrum or think of some scientific hypothesis as if it were a final conclusion. We must prove all things and hold fast that which is good.

The most amazing and revolutionary fact about the Kingdom of God is that it is a Kingdom of Love. As we have seen in an earlier chapter, the conception of a love-governed world, if practiced, would turn the world upside down, and yet that is what Jesus came to do. The principles on which His Kingdom is built—the principles of charity, kindness; love not only to friends but to enemies, love in answer to hate and anger—these, to anyone who does not change his natural mind and outlook, seem to be an impossibility. And yet, when it is considered, a world governed upon such principles would naturally be a happy one.

But is the conception of the human race as the family of God only the dream of a good man? To believe in its possibility is to find the Kingdom of God; to seek that Kingdom is the first priority of the Christian appeal. The one hope of its realization is that Jesus Himself lives to guide His people. Have we ever realized how the whole life of Jesus was an exemplification of love in opposition to every earthly and hellish force? 'Love came down at Christmas', as the beautiful hymn of Christina Rossetti says. When the mission of Incarnate Love on earth began it commenced with the declaration of the good news that God in His power had made an irruption into the world which was manifest through the activity of His finger in deeds of healing mercy. God sent His Son into the world because He loved it, not to judge, but to save. The love of humanity, not merely abstract humanity, but the love of individual men and women and little children with whom Jesus came in contact, is the Gospel account of his whole life. The apparent defeat of Jesus on Calvary was a great illusion because love triumphed over death, and indeed the Cross of Christ became a magnet and draws all men to it. The Gospel then that we have to offer is the Gospel of personal redemption and world salvation.

The responsibility of the Church of Christ, which in some sense is the visible Kingdom of God, the body of people who profess to follow the leadership of Christ, is a very heavy one. When we talk of the Church of Christ we must not think of those who profess and call themselves Christian, but who do not express the spirit of Christ, and the man who has not that spirit, says St Paul, is none of His. Throughout the centuries there have always been multitudes of people who were the true followers of the Saviour and who have commended His love by their life and words to the world. That our Lord should deign to use imperfect men and women must often have surprised His followers, but he does deign to use them and even prayed for us just before His Crucifixion.

One thing in the Church of today must be faced and overcome. I mean the divisions of Christianity. The Church which preaches the Gospel of a Kingdom of Love and believes in its heart that there is no solution for the world troubles except that which Christianity offers, must be made to realize that these divisions startlingly contradict the principles for which the Kingdom of Christ stands. Most of the divisions of Christianity, Zernov[1] argues, are expressions not of differences about truth, but of bad temper. He thinks that the doctrinal differences have been formulated to justify separation much more often than have been the causes of separation. I believe this to be profoundly true, although perhaps Zernov somewhat overstates his case. It is not so much by adaptations of ecclesiastical differences that this disastrous problem can be solved, but by mutual love to be found and shared in the Cross of Christ.

Our twofold gospel includes the message of the old Evangelism. 'Him who cometh to me, I will in no wise cast out' can never be superseded. To forget or ignore it is to forget that the modern man has something about him more fundamental than his modernism. In fifty years' time, it is quite likely that the so-called modern views of today will be superseded by new fashions;

[1] See *The Reintegration of the Church*.

but the fundamental needs of human nature will not change. Any Gospel that overlooks the ruin that sin brings to human beings, is incapable of bringing home to the heart of men the essential truths of Christianity. We must never forget that the actual appeals of Jesus were made to individuals. Always He was the Good Shepherd seeking the lost sheep, the one sheep over whose return to the fold the angels of Heaven rejoice, more than over the ninety-and-nine. And the awakening of the conscience of people who satisfy themselves with the material things of life, must be a central object of all evangelization. At the same time, the world needs the whole Gospel and not part of it—the Gospel of Jesus which is the Good News of the Kingdom of God, as well as the Good News that Jesus is a Saviour of individuals.

There are dangers, actually fallen into in recent years, of so emphasizing the social teaching of Jesus as to ignore His individual appeal. While therefore it is of imperative importance to teach that the Gospel of Jesus must be implemented by social reconstruction, and by the breaking down and conquest of all forces, national and international, which degrade human beings, His appeal to the individual man and the salvation that He gives to everyone who with penitence turns to Him, is of central importance. Indeed, nothing is more important to remember than that 'the soul of all improvement is the improvement of the soul', or as Mrs Browning put it first:

> *it takes a soul*
> *To raise a body even to a cleaner sty*

This book deals rather with the message than the methods of evangelism, but the problem of how the Church is to get over its message to the pagan England in which we live obviously necessitates some treatment of method. Our marching orders are to preach the Gospel to every creature, but how can we preach it to the people who will not listen—to people who are not so much hostile to what we have to say, but entirely indifferent?

We have to preach the Gospel to the people who do not want

to hear it, who do not and will not come to our churches. The difficulty is to find neutral ground on which the Church can meet the outsider. In my early ministry such ground was found in the public halls and theatres that we hired. Our Central Halls were called halls instead of churches because we wanted to reach the people who would not go to church, and we were in a large measure successful, as previous chapters of this book have shown.

Nowadays people have learnt that a Methodist Central Hall is only a church with another name. There seems nothing left for us but the open-air. If the people will not come to us, we must go to them in order to carry out the command of Jesus. But even then something else is wanted. A psychological as well as a local common platform is necessary. The great triumphs of early Methodism were in the open-air, but the beliefs common to the Wesleys and to the people of eighteenth-century England are no longer common to the Church and to the outsider, and methods such as those of the Salvation Army are no longer effective. A purely religious Service in the open-air will attract religious people to some extent, but at most only a few stragglers from the outside public.

In my early ministry I found a common platform not only in a secular hall but in common aspirations for the betterment of the people. Many of those aspirations today have been realized with the consequence that the outlook of the outsider no longer gives this common platform. Ways must be devised to overcome this difficulty. It has been overcome by the open-air forum of Dr Soper in what he calls 'fellowship of controversy'. Here the exponent of Christianity talks in the language of the people and strives to think in their modes of thought. The use of cinema and radio may well be developed as neutral ground for the evangelist and the outsider.

Generally speaking, the important training given to ministers in theological colleges is a training in the language of Israel, and the mode of thinking, essential as it is for a Christian minister, is not one intelligible to the pagan outsider of modern days.

Difficult though it may be, nothing is more necessary than training in the language of the people whom we have to reach. A missionary in a foreign country necessarily learns the language of its natives. We must realize the missionary obligations of the Church in a country so largely pagan as is ours. The open forum seems the best method at present of reaching the masses, particularly the intelligent masses, of the people of this country.

Important as evangelical campaigns are, and collective evangelism is—and it is with such evangelism that we are particularly concerned in this book—we must not imagine that this is the only way of reaching the people. We do well to remember the continuous witness of the Church to Christianity. Is there anything more impressive in the world than the continuous witness of the Church in its eucharistic worship to the pardoning death and saving life of Jesus? The Christian everywhere, however different his ritual and even his form of creed may be, makes his witness to the vital necessity of Christ—a world-wide witness—a persistent witness—ever showing forth the death of the Lord till He come, and, paradoxical though it may seem, ever announcing His abiding presence amongst His people.

But not only does the Church make this witness, it creates and feeds the evangelist. There can be no divorce between the Church and evangelism. There is no more mistaken notion than that of a gospel without a Church. Nothing is more important for the evangelist than worship. I cannot emphasize too often the fact, stressed in the first chapter of this book, of the sound doctrinal basis and eucharistic practice of the first decade of triumphant evangelism in the eighteenth century.

The responsibility of the Church to its Lord is in some ways a very terrible one, but it must be faced. The Church must realize that it has not completed its duty by sending out evangelists unless it is prepared to educate and to give a home to those whom the evangelist reaches. One of the tragical things in the evangelism of the past has been the high rate of infant mortality amongst those who profess to be born again. This is no modern complaint. My grandfather, for instance, who was one of the most successful evangelists in nineteenth-century Methodism, told my father that in his opinion not more than ten per cent of the converts made through Methodist evangelism endured faithful.

Modern evangelists have often complained that the results of their work have been lost through the incapacity of the Church to keep the people whom they gained. Certain questions of the President of the Methodist Conference recently published demand an answer from every Methodist church. They are as follows:

(1) Is your church *ready* to receive outsiders?
(2) Are the members a worshipping community, disciplined and informed in the arts of devotion and prayer?
(3) Can you make good to them the claim that the Church is the Body of Christ and, most of all, that in God's House God comes to us as He does nowhere else?

But important as mass evangelism is and evangelistic campaigns are, important as it is that the Church of Christ should take the offensive in the battle with evil, perhaps the most important of all forms of evangelism is the evangelism that cannot be organized, the witness of the individual to individuals, not only by word, but by quality of life. In the early days of Christianity when modern campaigns would have been impossible, Christianity won her victories not merely through the preaching of outstanding personalities, like St Paul, but by the higher quality of life of Christian people.

Dr T. R. Glover says that Christianity won its victories by out-thinking and outliving the paganism of the day. Let no one underestimate the value of Christian thinking—but ultimately it was Christian living that mattered most. A great Methodist authority once said that the genius of the Methodist people was best expressed in a single line of one of Charles Wesley's hymns:

*O let me commend my Saviour to you.*

CHRISTIAN ANSWER TO MODERN CHALLENGE 131

These people so realized Christ and the benefits that they received from Him that they could not be silent. They sang,

> *My heart is full of Christ, and longs*
> *Its glorious matter to declare—*

and their radiant lives illustrated and even illuminated their testimony.

We have today to make a relatively contented people discontented. It is only people who are convinced that Christianity gives them something that nothing else can give them who will convince others. With our enlarged views of the Gospel we have a richer message to give than even our fathers gave—not only that Christ satisfies us, but that His Kingdom of love and truth is the only thing that can solve the troubles of the world. This dominating faith even of simple people is the greatest of all means of evangelization. Its testimony is one that must be made from individual to individual in the shop, the school, the office, the ordinary walks of life. The work may often seem slow and unsensational, but it has won many victories in the past and will win them again. We need a Christian 'Fifth Column' infiltrating into every side of the life of our day. To my mind there are few passages of Scripture more moving than that of the account of the mission of the Seventy who were probably quite commonplace people, who went forth just obeying the word of Jesus, and who came to Him with joyous faces and voices saying that even the devils were subject to them in His name. Can we wonder that it was then that our Lord had that extraordinary vision when He said: 'I saw Satan falling as lightning from heaven.' The multiplied testimony and obedience of people to whom Jesus Christ is the supreme Reality is capable of making that vision able to be realized today.

The victory that overcomes the world is the victory of the faith that Jesus, the crucified Artisan, is the Son of God. We should not think of the term, 'Son of God', as a mere theological formula. It is the belief that He is supreme—*that* assures us of final victory. Living faith, founded on experience, enriched by knowledge, expressing itself in unwavering confidence, is the great need of the day, and yet must not we ponder those terrible and haunting words of Jesus: 'Shall the Son of Man, when He comes, find faith on the earth?'

Many discouragements have befallen earnest Christian workers today. Some people, as they see our empty churches, are in danger of despair. Let them never forget that the Church is the one institution which has outlasted the ancient world. For two thousand years the gates of Hell have failed to prevail against it. The vitality of the Church, because of the vitality of its risen Lord, is unconquerable. John Bunyan had something to say to his age about Giant Despair which has its significance for our own days. When Christian and Hopeful, having strayed from the highway, chose Bye-path Meadow, they were captured and imprisoned by Giant Despair. After some time they remembered the key called Promise with which the prison doors could be opened. That key is available to us today and the promise is: 'The kingdoms of this world shall become the kingdom of our God and of his Christ.'

But if we, like the later pilgrims, have not forsaken the highway, we may recall the campaign which Mr Great-heart organized against Giant Despair. First let it be noted that he did not put Mr Feeblemind and Mr Ready-to-Halt in the front line of the battle. He left them to look after the women and children. Here I think we can see a smile on John Bunyan's face when he suggests that Feeblemind was to look after Christiana. Obviously, she was much more capable of looking after him but she was gracious enough to let him think that he was in charge. I am sure, however, that she kept her eyes wide open.

Too often in our days Mr Feeblemind and Mr Ready-to-Halt have been the leaders in evangelical campaigns. Mr Ready-to-Halt has been very cautious but his progress naturally has been rather slow; and people like Mr Feeblemind 'who do not like laughter' and 'avoid doubtful disputations' are useless against the modern scientifically trained mind and the Communist. Still, something must be found for poor old Feeblemind and

Ready-to-Halt to do—after all they were good Christians—but not leadership of a campaign. Seniority and decrepitude are useless for campaigning. What then of the campaign? The leader, Mr Greatheart, a typical Englishman, strong in common sense but always kindly and tender even to the feeble-minded, has as his companion Mr Honest, 'a cock of the right sort', a citizen, notwithstanding his unfortunate birthplace, of the Kingdom of Truth. The only reason that Valiant-for-Truth was absent from the campaign is that he joined the pilgrim band later. But most important of all is the fact that the four boys were there—the total youth of the pilgrim band. The courage and hope of youth are and always must be the guarantee of victory. Of course the band was unconquerable! Giant Despair and his wife, Diffidence, were decapitated: the castle was demolished and the prisoners liberated. What a welcome the campaigners received when they returned! Even Ready-to-Halt and Feeblemind, we are told, were 'merry and jocund', and the whole pilgrim band burst out into music and dancing. In this spirit the campaign today must be fought and won. Youth may go forth with confidence and song. What better song than—

*Rejoice, the Lord is King!*
*Your Lord and King adore;*

*Lift up your heart, lift up your voice;*
*Rejoice; again I say, Rejoice.*

CHAPTER TWELVE

# 'ATTEND THE TRUMPET'S SOUND!'

*O for a trumpet voice,*
  *On all the world to call!*
*To bid their hearts rejoice*
  *In Him who died for all:*
*For all my Lord was crucified,*
*For all, for all my Saviour died.*

*Hark, how the watchmen cry!*
  *Attend the trumpet's sound!*
*Stand to your arms, the foe is nigh,*
  *The powers of hell surround:*
*Who bow to Christ's command,*
  *Your arms and hearts prepare!*
*The day of battle is at hand!*
  *Go forth to glorious war!*

*Jesu's tremendous name*
  *Puts all our foes to flight:*
*Jesus, the meek, the angry Lamb,*
  *A Lion is in fight.*

THE TERM 'Salvation Army', as I said in Chapter 8, expresses well the exterior activities of the Catholic Church. This name expresses effectively the cause for which the Church fights—the salvation of men. The Church is militant but not military. A distinguished pacifist of my acquaintance once said that the only militarism left in him was the militant hymns of the Church. He could not do without their martial music. The Church of Christ marches out to certain victory. Every member of it is a conscript in the army of Christ. It marches through the centuries to triumph over the difficulties that beset it, often baffled, in all the centuries more or less divided, but never beaten, for the gates of Hell cannot prevail against it. This army of the Living God remains today the one historical institution with nineteen centuries of life and activity behind it. The work of Christians in every century is to extend the Kingdom of Christ, to win back for God dominion in every area of human life from the forces of evil. The earth is the Lord's and the fullness thereof, and the Devil and his hosts are impertinent intruders to be driven out by the armies of the Lamb.

We may well use the names 'Principalities and Powers' by which St Paul catalogued the spiritual forces as he saw them, in that demon-haunted world, to describe the forces of evil in our own days. Battle against these forces was never more needed, but final victory of the soldiers of Christ is assured to them by the words: 'Fear not little flock, for it is your Father's good pleasure to give you the Kingdom.'

We must not, however, be misled by military metaphors. The army of Christ is the strangest that the world has ever seen. It is a flock of sheep, and a flock of sheep is apparently the least military description imaginable of an Army. And yet the forces we have to fight against have never been more menacing than in these days.

This is the hour and power of materialistic science. A few years ago leading scientists more than once informed the world that if only people would leave science alone, the scientists would create an earthly paradise. But no earthly paradise can meet the needs of those in whose hearts God hath set eternity; but the materialistic way of thinking still persists. Communism has been called a Christian heresy. The Apocalyptic dreams of fanatics of earlier times have been applied to the future of this earth rather than to a heaven in the skies. They have dreamt of a new earth, but discarded the old heaven. They set their hopes upon a future of human happiness, by mere materialistic development, for people who reject God disbelieve in the soul and renounce immortality as a fantastic dream. This materialistic view of human nature in reality degrades it so that men are regarded as nothing more than the highest of animals instead of being the children of God. This widespread materialism, of which Communism is only one expression, is the evil against which the modern Church must make unrelenting war. The materialism, which bases the future of the human race on the rejection of God and spiritual life but promises to deluded people an almost celestial society here on earth, is really anti-Christ. Anti-Christ, when formidable, is not a repulsive demon. Satan's way is to make himself look like an angel of light. We are not 'ignorant of his devices'.

What then is the army which can contend successfully against such forces? It is a flock of sheep. This strange, unmilitary description of the Church of God is a vivid picture of the apparent weakness of the Church against the militant forces of the world. If we again refer to military metaphors, the comparison of sheep becomes the more forceful, and yet it is true as we often sing:

> *Like a mighty Army*
> *Moves the Church of God.*

What are the weapons of this mighty host? They are purely spiritual. The familiar recital of them in the Sixth Chapter of the Epistle to the Ephesians we all remember. The one offensive weapon is the Word of God which is the Sword of the Spirit. Truth is the girdle, peace the shoes, faith the shield, salvation the helmet, and righteousness the breastplate. Charles Wesley's paraphrase in his hymn 'Soldiers of Christ arise, and put your armour on' concludes with this notable couplet,

> *But arm yourselves with all the mind*
> *That was in Christ, your Head.*

This is really an admirable condensation in a single sentence of the armour with which Christians fight. Perhaps the rather different use of the metaphor in the first Epistle to the Thessalonians, though not so often quoted, is even more illuminating. The armour is there said to be the breastplate of Faith and Love and for an helmet the Hope of Salvation. Faith, Hope and

Charity, that is to say, the characteristic and indeed differentiating Christian virtues, are the weapons with which the Army, more truly even described as the Flock of the Good Shepherd contends with the forces of evil, and its encouragement is the assertion of Jesus that the Meek shall inherit the earth.

Is the Church of Christ awake today to the magnitude of the forces with which she must contend? Has there ever been a time in which it has been more necessary to awake from slumber and to arm herself with the armour of light? The forces with which she contends are unquestionably formidable; but 'Faith is a victory which overcomes the world'. Love in the long run conquers hate, and the hope of salvation is a spur to activity which encourages the Christian man. For having such a hope he will purify himself even as Christ is pure, knowing that when Christ shall appear he shall be like Him, for he shall see Him as He is.

While we must not underestimate the formidable character of the threat of materialism to mankind, it is easy for us to overestimate the menace with which we are threatened. Materialistic communism can never permanently satisfy the hungry souls of men. Few books more illuminating have lately been published than that written by disillusioned communists entitled, *The God that Failed*. These men, some of them well-known and distinguished persons, were inspired between the two world wars by the vision of a happy world where class distinctions would be abolished and the disinherited masses of people would enjoy the privileges of emancipated humanity; but actual experience of the intolerable discipline of communist rule brought about their disillusionment, so that though it was in some sense a grief to them all, they were compelled to renounce a system which was really a new form of human slavery. Mr Bertrand Russell's fear of a scientific society lacking in love, referred to earlier, finds a vivid expression in the brilliant satires of Mr Aldous Huxley, repulsive in some ways as they are. It is mockery indeed to call the exclusively scientific society of the future as he projects it 'a brave new world'.

In the long run no weapons will prove as effective, and indeed often in the past have proved their effectiveness, as 'The mind of Christ, Faith, Hope, and Charity'. For, recurring to the figure of the 'flock', we need to remember that the great Shepherd of the flock is Himself the Lamb that was slain. The Lamb of God died on the Cross of Calvary and was buried; but when the God of Peace brought Him again from the Dead, the Lamb was the Great Shepherd of the Sheep—as we read in Revelation $7^{17}$: 'For the Lamb which is in the midst of the throne shall feed them, and shall lead them unto living fountains of waters.' The Lamb, that is to say, is the Shepherd who leads His sheep into green pastures beside still waters. The actual figure of the shepherd is brought out more graphically in Dr Moffatt's translation:

> *for the Lamb in the midst of the*
> *throne will be their shepherd,*
> *guiding them to fountains of*
> *living water.*

The fact that our Leader and Shepherd is a Lamb determines the nature of Christian warfare. Whether Pacifism is accepted or rejected in national and international relations, one thing is perfectly certain, the Church can fight only with the weapons of Faith, Hope, and Charity. No greater tragedies in the history of the Church have occurred than the mistaken use of military weapons to support the Church of God. But while we are inspired by the lowliness and humility of the Lamb who is our Shepherd, we must not forget that such a thing exists as the Wrath of the Lamb. Let not that wrath ever be confused in our minds with mere ill-temper or fury. The wrath of the Lamb is the Love of Christ blazing with fiery indignation against those, and especially against those, who corrupt and hurt his little ones. And while it is too easy for Christians to imagine their mere ill-temper to be the wrath of the Lamb, it is also true that an indignation with evil, blazing like the fiery love of God into flame, should characterize our Christian conflict. We are told to be angry and sin not. This is a difficult duty to carry out, but it is necessary to remember that there are circumstances under which we sin if we are not angry. There are limits to Christian toleration, we must be hostile toward all the forces which degrade human beings, and, however inconvenient and painful it may be to us, we are compelled by our vocation as the soldiers of Christ to do all in our power to undermine the crashing evils of today which debase and exploit human beings.

To follow the Lamb whithersoever He leadeth us is not always to feed in green pastures or to be refreshed with the waters of comfort; but to follow Him into the valleys of the shadow of death, into perilous places. His kingdom is a kingdom of truth as well as of love, and we must not fear truth. Perhaps the best thing which T. S. Huxley ever said was that the scientist must sit down before fact like a little child. That certainly is the attitude of Christ, whose Kingdom is not of this world, as He told Pontius Pilate, but a kingdom of truth. The Church has been too afraid of new discoveries of Truth, and too often has little realized that it is truth that makes us free. In His conflict with the Devil in the hours of His temptation in the wilderness, our Lord overcame the Evil One with the Sword of the Spirit, the Word of God, the Eternal Truth. It is extraordinary how often new discoveries in the scientific world, which have frightened Christians because they challenge some point of their creed, have proved in the long run to establish rather than to destroy their faith. This does not mean that we are to accept with a credulous spirit every new statement of modern science, but it does mean that we need not fear Truth, because Christ's Kingdom is a Kingdom of Truth. We have to follow our Lord into dangerous places. Sheep it is true are the most timid of creatures, but the Great Shepherd of the Sheep ever lives in His flock; not only to lead but to guide and guard His little ones. Nothing is more needed in the days in which we live, than simple courage. Courage is the expression of true faith. Jesus was never afraid of the Devil, why should we who follow Him be? We need to sing the triumphant hymn of Martin Luther:

> *And were this world all devils o'er,*
> *And watching to devour us,*
> *We lay it not to heart so sore;*
> *Not they can overpower us,*
>   *And let the Prince of ill*
>   *Look grim as e'er he will,*
> *He harms us not a whit;*
> *For why? His doom is writ;*
> *A word shall quickly slay him.*

Why is the Church of God today so often on the defensive? Why do not we realize that the best defensive is the offensive? It is not sufficient for Christians to say:

> *I shall be safe; for Christ displays*
> *Superior power and guardian grace.*

We are called to fight the enemy on his own grounds. Of the Church we read that the gates of Hell shall not prevail against her. It must be difficult for the 'gates of Hell', if the metaphor can be followed, to find their way to the rock on which the Church is built. We need to fight our battle with evil at Hell gate. How many Christians today take the offensive and march to the gates of Hell for combat with the Devil? Are we not too smug and contented with ourselves? Are we not always seeking as it were shell-holes and dug-outs to avoid the artillery of the evil one? And a new and courageous attack on the forces of evil is what we are called to:

> *Hark, how the watchmen cry!*
> *Attend the trumpet's sound!*

Do many people today read Olive Schreiner? Some of her dreams are well worth our perusal. A pioneer for women's rights and liberties, she once wrote a dream to sustain her views which can well be applied to Christian campaigns:

I thought I stood in Heaven before God's throne, and God asked me what I had come for. I said I had come to arraign my brother, Man.

God said: 'What has he done?'

I said: 'He has taken my sister, Woman, and has stricken her, and wounded her, and thrust her out into the streets; she lies there prostrate. His hands are red with blood. *I* am here to arraign him; that the kingdom be taken from him, because he is not worthy, and given unto me. My hands are pure.'

I showed them.

God said: 'Thy hands are pure.—Lift up thy robe.'

I raised it; my feet were red, blood red, as if I had trodden in wine.

God said: 'How is this?'

I said: 'Dear Lord, the streets on earth are full of mire. If I should walk straight on in them my outer robe might be bespotted, you see how white it is! Therefore I pick my way.'

God said: '*On what?*'

I was silent, and I let my robe fall. I wrapped my mantle about my head. I went out softly. I was afraid that the angels would see me.

Once more I stood at the gate of Heaven, I and another. We held fast by one another; we were very tired. We looked up at the great gates; the angels opened them, and we went in. The mud was on our garments. We walked across the marble floor, and up to the great throne. Then the angels divided us. Her, they set upon the top step, but me, upon the bottom; for, they said: 'Last time this woman came here she left red foot-marks on the floor; we had to wash them out with our tears. Let her not go up.'

Then she, with whom I came, looked back, and stretched out her hand to me; and I went and stood beside her. And the angels, they, the shining ones who never sinned and never suffered, walked by us to and fro and up and down; I think we should have felt a little lonely there if it had not been for one another, the angels were so bright.

God asked me what I had come for; and I drew my sister forward a little that he might see her.

God said: 'How is it you are here together today?'

I said: 'She was upon the ground in the street, and they passed over her; I lay down by her, and she put her arms around my neck, and so I lifted her, and we two rose together.'

God said: 'Whom are you now come to accuse before me?'

I said: 'We are come to accuse no man.'

And God bent, and said: 'My children—what is it that ye seek?'

And she beside me drew my hand that I should speak for both.

I said: 'We have come to ask that thou shouldst speak to Man, our brother, and give us a message for him that he might understand, and that he might——'

God said: 'Go, take the message down to him!'

I said: 'But what *is* the message?'

God said: 'Upon your hearts it is written; take it down to him.'

And we turned to go; the angels went with us to the door. They looked at us.

And one said—'Ai! but their dresses are beautiful!'

And the other said: 'I thought it was mire when they came in, but see, it is all golden!'

But another said: 'Hush, it is the light from their faces!'

And we went down to him.

The Church is a Salvation Army. She is here to carry out the work of rescuing the perishing, of saving souls of men. It is little use merely to fulminate against social evils, especially as when, like the woman in Olive Schreiner's dreams, we, however unconsciously, profit from them. Something more is required of us than the preservation of respectability. We must go down if necessary into the gutter, to the very gates of Hell, to follow the Great Shepherd in seeking and saving the lost. Do we really suppose that the Church of Christ, except in a few of its prophets and martyrs, is carrying out the great offensive into which the trumpet of God calls?

We, who are the soldiers of Christ, are citizens of His Kingdom, a kingdom which is not of this world. British Colonists have girdled the world with little Englands, so it is given to us to girdle the world with little Heavens, if we are true patriots and soldiers of the Kingdom of Christ. Armed with Faith, Hope, and Love, we can be more than conquerors with Him that hath loved us.

> *Our Captain leads us on;*
> *He beckons from the skies.*
>
> *Jesu's tremendous name*
> *Puts all our foes to flight:*
> *Jesus, the meek, the angry Lamb,*
> *A Lion is in fight.*
> *By all hell's host withstood,*
> *We all hell's host o'erthrow;*
> *And conquering them, through Jesu's blood,*
> *We still to conquer go.*

ADDITIONAL NOTE

# ESCHATOLOGY AND APOCALYPTIC

IN HIS RECENT book, *Theology of the New Testament*, Professor Bultmann does not admit Dodd's interpretation. He would allow, in a sense, 'the Kingdom of God is dawning', 'is about to come', to be the meaning of our Lord's words; but he says quite plainly: 'All that does not mean that God's reign is already here, but it does mean that it is dawning.' He thinks of the coming of the Kingdom as a future event with such cosmic consequences as those detailed in Mark 13, whereas Dodd, I am sure rightly, says that in Christ the Kingdom of God has come and that the finger of God was actually at work in the miracles which He was performing. Bultmann's view is that the coming of the Son of Man in Judgement was an event which Jesus expected would take place in the immediate future; but the heavenly visitor—the expected—the Son of Man, is not Jesus Himself, but one for whom Jesus looks. The identification of Jesus with the Son of Man according to Bultmann was made after His Resurrection by His Disciples, who then thought that He had ascended into Heaven to come back again as the Son of Man in Judgement. Bultmann gives no proof whatever of his views, and makes no examination of the meaning of the Greek words with which Dodd so effectively deals.[1] He dismisses as legend the narratives which would seem to support Dodd's views, that Jesus Himself actually used, as descriptive of Himself, the term 'Son of Man'. It is unlikely that this identification would ever have been disputed except by extreme eschatologists who find it destructive of their theory.

If we accept as an objective and accurate interpretation, as we do accept it, Dodd's demonstration that eschatology was

[1] See p. 54, *supra*.

actually realized, it is unnecessary to criticize the details of Bultmann's assertions.

Many early Christians undoubtedly looked for the speedy return of Jesus to judgement and the end of all things. Dr C. H. Dodd writes, in some recent lectures:

'A certain tension can be discerned in almost all parts of the New Testament; the Kingdom of God will come; it has come; Christ has come; Christ will come. This tension is something which is inseparable from the thought of early Christianity. But whichever way you look at it, it meant that Christians were living in a unique period of history. There had never been anything like it before, and there would not be anything like it again, because, through what had happened, human life had acquired a fresh dimension, and the powers of a world beyond had made impact upon human life in this world.'[2]

'For some, this great event was the absolute end of history, after which nothing at all would happen. It would be succeeded by some form of existence totally different from anything that we can either experience or imagine. For others, it was the beginning of a new age of history in which the power of God would be signally at work.'[3]

The unique character of the experiences of Christians in the first century is a fact of outstanding importance. In no age have people been so aware of the Eternal Order. The Glory of God broke through and men experienced for themselves the working of the 'finger of God' in the miracles of mercy wrought by Jesus. 'The Kingdom of God was upon them.' Not only did an experience of God's immediate presence break on them through the works of Christ, but His person was a manifestation of the Divine Glory which filled them, as St Mark shows, with reverent awe and fear. In the Johannine writings at the end of the century this sense of awe and wonder is preserved in such words as 'That which was from the beginning, which we have heard, which we have seen with our eyes, which we have looked upon, and our hands have handled, of the Word of life'.

[2, 3] See C. H. Dodd, *Gospel and Law*.

What wonder there is in the great and familiar statement: 'We beheld His glory, glory as of the only begotten Son of God, full of grace and truth.' Moments like those of the Transfiguration dazzled and bewildered the men who experienced them. The tragedy of Calvary which plunged them into despair was followed by a quick revulsion of feeling on Easter morning, when they began to realize that what had seemed to be defeat and disaster, in reality was the triumph of love; and the thorn-crowned head of Calvary they realized was crowned with glory and honour. Then the further experience of Pentecost when they were overwhelmed by the powers of the world to come was the culmination of a series of experiences unique and unprecedented of the actual irruption of the Eternal Order in time and space. It is indeed difficult for us to realize the tremendous effect of experiences so unexpected but in many ways puzzling to the generation that underwent them.

Dr Dodd's phrase 'Realized Eschatology' can be applied to the Day of Pentecost as truly as to the early events to which he applied it. These extraordinary experiences of the Eternal were only partially explicable at the time of their occurrence, and the expectation that such unique events would be followed by that consummation of all things predicted by the ancient Prophets and symbolized by contemporary Apocalyptists was not unnatural.

In Bultmann's pamphlet, much discussed in Germany, *The Demythologizing of the New Testament*, there is much that English Evangelical Christians would reject; but his characterization of Apocalyptic as a myth is undoubtedly fair. There can be no doubt that Apocalyptic is symbolical. Indeed, as Daniel himself says, his visions are visions of the night. That is to say, they are of dream texture. All dream language is symbolical. In this a modern psychologist, Dr Rivers, is in agreement with such interpreters of dreams as Joseph and Daniel. The literal interpretation which has been given, and is still given by many English Christians, to Apocalyptic revelations is obviously wrong. No doubt the Jewish myth was an instrument of conveying truth to Jewish minds, and sometimes we find in such books as those of Daniel and the Revelation, clues by which these myths can be interpreted, especially when they are a figurative expression of historical events. But when speculations about the future are written in Apocalyptic language, we have no way of testing their truth or of really understanding their meaning. Jewish Apocalyptic never seems to have been intelligible to other peoples. Scholars like C. H. Dodd, T. R. Glover, and even Albert Schweitzer (himself an eschatologist) emphasize the amazing difference between the Jewish mentality and that of the other nations of the Hellenistic world.[4] Schweitzer himself claims that eschatological Apocalyptic is not only an unintelligible medium of thought to the modern Western mind, but needed in the first century interpretation for the understanding of the Mediterranean world generally. He claims that the Johannine writings were such an interpretation.

This seems, as we read it, to be an illuminating statement. Anyhow, it is quite clear that the thought-forms in the fourth Gospel are those of the Greek rather than the Hebrew mentality. Dr Dodd in his new commentary on St John has shown the correspondence between the language of the Hermetic writings and those of St John. It must be remembered, notwithstanding the many difficulties as to the authorship of the fourth Gospel, that it was written at least two generations after the death of Jesus. A general consensus of opinion today seems to be that whoever wrote it in its present form, it contains the testimonies of an eye-witness. That this eye-witness was the Beloved Apostle cannot be regarded as disproved. But in any case we have in this Gospel the results of many years of reflection on the life, teaching, and death of Jesus.

It is quite noteworthy that Apocalyptic almost disappears in this Gospel; terms familiar in Greek philosophy take the place of the imagery of the Jewish prophets.

The difficulty for us today is that Jesus seems sometimes to have used this Apocalyptic language. It is true that scholars, even such an eschatological scholar as Schweitzer, think that the

[4] See Schweitzer, *The Mysticism of Paul the Apostle*, pp. 376-96.

so-called little Apocalypse of Mark 13 has in it only a few sayings of Jesus. Yet He did use words such as those He spoke to the High Priest at His trial. According to St Mark He said: 'Ye shall see the Son of Man sitting on the right hand of Power and coming on the clouds of Heaven.' In Luke and Matthew it is notable that both of them, though they use rather different Greek words, say that Jesus said *'Henceforth'* or *'From this time forth* ye shall see the Son of Man'. It seems reasonable to deduce from this that, though our Lord used the current Apocalyptic language when he spoke of the spectacle of the Son of Man seated on a cloud, he could not have meant these words to be taken literally, or he would not have said *'From now onward'* or 'henceforth'. When we remember that these Gospels could not have been written in their present form until fifty years after the death of Christ, it seems clear that the writers would hardly have recorded these words unless the claim that Jesus made had been actually verified, and this can only be true if he was speaking in metaphor of the triumphs which He accomplished through His death and resurrection.

The expectation of the final consummation of all things which dominated the minds of many, under the influence of Apocalyptic visions, is not surprising. But what seems difficult to understand is that people with such an outlook should at the same time have done everything in their power to extend the Kingdom of God on earth. Gradually, of course, the fact that Jesus did not come again to judgement as they expected made them realize that they had entered into a new epoch—the epoch of the Kingdom of Christ upon earth. They realized more and more that the Kingdom of God which had broken upon them was a Kingdom that had come to stay. Their Lord and Master, who had died for their sins, had risen again and promised to be with them always in their efforts to extend His Kingdom. They were to join with Him in battling and conquering Principalities and Powers. Their warfare was to be with no carnal weapons, but with that love shed abroad in their hearts by the Holy Spirit. Faith, love and hope were their weapons.

No doubt this Kingdom of Christ on earth implies our acceptance of the Doctrine of Realized Eschatology, which as we have seen in previous pages was the genuine experience of early Christians.

The acceptance of a distinction between the Kingdom of God in its universal scope, and the Kingdom of Christ as a historical Kingdom on earth, is not only the natural deduction from the doctrine of Realized Eschatology, but a solution of problems that arise in the interpretation of the term 'Kingdom'.

At the end of the first century, the Apocalyptic expression, 'henceforth ye shall see the Son of Man coming in clouds', finds confirmation in such words as these in the victory that 'overcometh the world, even our faith'. Who is he that overcometh the world, but he that believeth that Jesus is the Son of God. That this man will be proved to be the *Son of God* is what Apocalyptic visions of that day strove to assert. It is evident that John's Epistle makes the same claim.

www.ingramcontent.com/pod-product-compliance
Lightning Source LLC
Chambersburg PA
CBHW050824160426
43192CB00010B/1888